Aspects

of the

Analysis of

Family

Structure

Aspects

ANSLEY J. COALE

of the

LLOYD A. FALLERS

Analysis of

MARION J. LEVY, JR.

Family

DAVID M. SCHNEIDER

Structure

SILVAN S. TOMKINS

PRINCETON, NEW JERSEY

PRINCETON UNIVERSITY PRESS

1965

To the memory of

F. F. GREENMAN

to Whom Many
an Education is Owed

". . . *when Bill Guthrie, umpiring in the American League, called a third strike on Wes Ferrell, a good pitcher and dangerous hitter with the Cleveland Indians, Ferrell heaved his stick into the air.*

" 'If dat bat comes down,' said Mr. Guthrie, not wishing to be hasty about it, 'you're outta d' ball game.' "

Quoted from "Views of Sports,"
Red Smith, *New York Herald Tribune*,
Friday, April 25, 1952.

CONTENTS

PREFACE

THIS IS an essay in hypotheses with some critical comments. I have presented it in this form without any attempt at large scale empirical verification of its hypotheses because I believe that the primary goal of the scientific game is highly generalized systems of theory. I believe it is more important that hypotheses (or theories) be fruitful for the development of yet further ones than that they be right. I believe that one of the most fundamental rules of the scientific game is the principle of parsimony and that strategies of analysis should be devised with this in mind. This essay is an attempt to come to far-reaching conclusions in the field of family analysis in terms of a small number of variables. I hope and believe that these hypotheses are important for the following reason: they are so posed that from either their verification or disproof we shall know a great deal more than we know now.

More specifically I have tried to show the following: 1) It is possible to come to conclusions that are not banally true by definition and that apply to any society anywhere at any time; 2) that systematic use of the distinction between ideal and actual structures (or patterns) is one of the most powerful theoretical tools of the social scientist; 3) that neglect of biological factors—doubtless related to a fine reaction against naïve forms of biological determinism—has been a serious mistake in the strategy of social science; 4) that the uses of the implications of demographic findings are much too important and fruitful for all of us to be left solely to demographers; 5) that

Preface

most extant descriptions of ideal kinship and family structures are inconsistent with possible actual structures if accurate, or they are untenable as descriptions of the ideal structures; and 6) that use of this sort of analysis can lead to new hypotheses, e.g., that suggested about the change with modernization to a preference for nuclear families as an ideal structure. (See pp. 56-60.)

In this effort Professor Ansley J. Coale of the Office of Population Research, Princeton University, supplied the basic demographic models used in the attempt to show that however great the variation in ideal structures might be, the variations in actual structures of kinship, insofar as kinship phenomena are in any way dependent upon such factors as the numbers of individuals present, age distribution, sex distribution, marital-spouse pair distributions, generational distributions, sibling distributions, etc., are not so great as most social scientists have tended to assume or imply. Professor David M. Schneider of the Department of Anthropology at the University of Chicago has attacked what he considers to be an overly biologistic orientation of the entire discussion. His attack is focused on the basic conceptual scheme used here. I do not believe that the element of biological orientation that he sees is in fact so extreme nor do I think it untenable to allege that all peoples do orient to biological factors to some extent. I certainly do not hold that kinship must be defined in this way—only that it is fruitful to define it in this way. I do not define it solely in biological terms but only as oriented in part to biological considerations. His commentary, however, represents an important point of view. I would not want these hypotheses published without someone raising the kind of questions he has raised.

Preface

Professor Lloyd A. Fallers, also of the Department of Anthropology at the University of Chicago, has raised a different kind of question. My hypotheses make assertions about any society, any time, anywhere—regardless of any known variations in social (or cultural?) structures (or patterns). Professor Fallers has shown that if *fictive* kinship is not limited in specific ways, my hypotheses do not necessarily hold. I do not happen to believe that the examples he cites are in fact genuine "exceptions to the rule" as I have posed it, nor do I believe my position has some of the implications he sees, but I deeply regret that I have no theoretical answer to the possibility he raises. I suspect that there are limits on the possible range of fictive kinship, but I have no good theoretical argument to this effect. Therefore, although I know of no empirical exception to the hypotheses as I have asserted them, Professor Fallers' point is a deadly and fruitful theoretical criticism. I wish that without the argument being tautological I could think of neither theoretical nor empirical exceptions to the propositions as posed.

Professor Silvan S. Tomkins' essay speaks eloquently for itself. In addition to its relevance here it makes available in abbreviated compass much of the core of concern of the two volumes so far published of his *Affect, Imagery, and Consciousness* (Springer Publishing Co., New York, 1962-63). I am in his debt in general for bringing that to bear on the subject of this volume. I am in his debt much more specifically for the far-reaching implications of his concept of and theories about affects. Whether tenable or not, his approach brings a new and fruitful point of view to the whole question of the role of "biological" factors and their interdependency with "social" ones. I accept wholeheartedly his criticism that even in my

Preface

care that biological factors not be overlooked, I have thought of them in terms of current clichés. I have left my statements as they were, however, because more is to be learned from his criticism of those positions than would be from the specific alterations I might currently be able to make to eliminate the relevance of his remarks.

The work begun here has only just begun. I hope that by the use of computers,[1] and with the assistance of demographers and others, I can explore what the range of actual variation is likely to be given different ideal kinship structures with regard to numbers of individuals present by contrast with numbers of generations represented, etc. In some of these factors actual variation is likely to be much greater than in others. For example, numbers of individuals will vary more with variations in ideal family structures than numbers of generations represented. Since variations in any other of the factors mentioned below (p. 41, fn. 33) always involve some variations in number of members, actual variations in any other category must, in some sense, be less than the variation in number of members. One thing, however, seems to me crystal clear: preoccupation with the extent of variation of ideal structures of kinship and

---

[1] It is a pleasure to be able to note that during last year Professors Kunstadter, Buhler, Stephan and Westoff of Princeton University collaborated in developing a program for testing out assumptions about ideal structures of cross-cousin marriage on a computer. It became quite obvious that no society could survive unless the actual structures diverge from what are generally described as the structures of cross-cousin marriage. See Peter Kunstadter, Roald Buhler, Frederick F. Stephan and Charles F. Westoff, "Demographic Variability and Preferential Marriage Patterns," *American Journal of Physical Anthropology*, N.S. Vol. 21, No. 4 (December 1963).

Preface

family structure have obscured some of the most important common features of all human life everywhere.

I owe a debt to the University environment here at Princeton which makes such researches possible. I owe a detailed debt to the National Science Foundation for time off from regular teaching duties and funds for secretarial assistance that made possible two years of productivity on which I shall always look back with nostalgia and envy. Among my departmental colleagues at Princeton I owe special debts to Peter Kunstadter, Wilbert E. Moore, Frederick F. Stephan and Maurice Zeitlin. I owe a debt to the graduate and undergraduate students with whom I have had the good fortune to be associated. Their willingness to listen to me and squabble with me has helped. I owe special debts of stimulation to Paul Bohannan and Andrew Effrat. I owe debts to my colleagues in and out of the social sciences. Dr. Roger S. Pinkham of Bell Laboratories has helped me in ways that defy identification. Finally, I am obliged to the Princeton University Press for the help and interest of Mr. David Harrop in seeing this effort to publication.

I hope these brief essays—with their disagreements left in—will encourage the kind of criticism that will make these hypotheses as questionable as I obdurately believe they make most descriptions of kinship in our literature.

Marion J. Levy, Jr.
*Woodrow Wilson School of Public
and International Affairs
Princeton University*

ASPECTS OF THE ANALYSIS
OF FAMILY STRUCTURE

MARION J. LEVY, JR.

INTRODUCTION

THE RELATED concepts of kinship structure and the family unit occupy an interesting position in the general field of social analysis. Few if any attempts to analyze societies neglect these concepts altogether. A considerable proportion of other social analysis is also focused on such matters. Still and all there is no modern attempt of any magnitude to produce a highly generalized treatment or exploration of these phenomena. The only close approaches to such treatment have focused overwhelmingly on the "relational aspects of kinship" and little if at all on the "membership units" as such.[1] Some of the most fruitful and interesting work in the field of anthropology has been based on this relational approach and preoccupation. The work on this score has on the whole achieved a much higher stage of general analytic treatment than even such popular concepts as "culture." With the notable exception of linguistics it almost certainly constitutes the most highly and rigorously developed field within the general area of social and/or cultural anthropology.

Among sociologists there is, of course, an enormous literature—an entire "field"—on the family. Much of this has been in terms of membership units

[1] Well known among such treatments is G. P. Murdock, *Social Structure,* Macmillan, New York, 1949. For a discussion of the "relationship" and "membership unit" approaches, see below, pp. 5-7.

Aspects of the Analysis of Family Structure

as such, but little of it has been aimed at very general levels. In recent years, especially, no other literature in sociology testifies more strongly to the preoccupation of a great number of sociologists with an extremely limited and special range of all the social materials of world history. Even apparently generalized treatments are likely to be narrowly focused on such specific cases as the modern American family. If the focus is more general, it rarely extends the treatment further than the limit of the type of family associated with relatively modernized societies. Actual references to more general levels are rare. The appearance of greater generality is largely a function of supplementary ad hoc remarks about other cases or by confusion of the specific case studied with the more general.[2]

There are good reasons to suggest that these concepts and their associated phenomena should occupy a more central role in our search for general systems of analysis and general theory. Before going into these matters, however, I should like to define the terms "kinship structure" and "family" as I shall use them. Kinship structure is defined as "that portion of the analytic and concrete structures of a society in terms of which, in addition to other orientations sometimes equally if not even more important, the membership of the units and the nature of the solidarity among the members of the units is determined by orientation to the facts of biological relatedness and/or sexual intercouse."[3] A family unit is defined

[2] See, for example, T. Parsons and R. F. Bales, *Family, Socialization and Interaction Process*, Free Press, Glencoe, 1955.

[3] Taken with slight modification from *The Structure of Society*, Princeton University Press, Princeton, 1952, p. 203. All concepts of structure and function, institutions, etc., as

Marion J. Levy, Jr.

as any membership unit of the kinship structure for which in addition to other orientations, sometimes equally if not more important for the members, the membership of the units and the nature of the solidarity among the members is determined by orientation to the facts of biological relatedness *and* sexual intercourse.[4]

---

used here are taken from that source unless otherwise defined or cited. *Fictive* kinship structures are defined as those in terms of which the orientation to biological relatedness and/or sexual intercourse is via simulation.

[4] One problem about this definition must be clarified here. The family unit is defined by the combination of orientations to descent *and* sexual intercourse. It in no way implies that sexual intercourse is the most important focus of a family as distinguished from a descent unit or any other. Indeed both family and descent units may have far greater emphases on descent or on something else altogether. The definition used here in no way implies that the "marital bond," i.e., the husband-wife solidarity takes precedence over others. It merely implies that no unit will be called a family unit without some orientation past, present, or future to sexual relationships among two or more of the members in addition to some orientation to descent. The importance of either or both orientations may vary greatly. Ordinarily I would expect both to be of considerable importance, but the range of variation even in this might be great.

There are many problems about this definition that need not detain us here. It should be obvious that with such a definition a single society may be characterized by several quite different types of family units. This is, of course, in addition to the distinction between the "family of orientation" and the "family of procreation." The flexibility or reference of this definition of the family concept is not without its disadvantages for analysis. At least, however, this strategy of definition does not predispose the analyst to fall implicitly into the assumption that each society has one and only one type of family (save for the orientation-procreation distinction). As a minimum the families of orientation and procreation—perhaps more than one of each—may be distinguished for all. Others may vary on various bases such as income,

Aspects of the Analysis of Family Structure

Given the two definitions stated above, one can, with relative precision of definition at least, distinguish four different types of concrete social structures of which three are kinship structures and the fourth is residually defined so as to encompass all other concrete structures. The three kinship structures are: 1) descent units (those oriented at least in part to biological relatedness but not to sexual intercourse); 2) non-family units oriented at least in part to sexual intercourse (perhaps a very special kind of kinship unit, not necessarily rare but ordinarily probably of short duration); and 3) family units. The non-kinship units constitute all concrete structures oriented to neither biological descent nor sexual intercourse. These distinctions may have some utility for general taxonomic purposes.[5] It

---

ethnic background, etc. No definition of the concept should make it easy to speak of *the* X (e.g., the *French*) family without having to establish the monolithic nature of the family structures concerned. See L. A. Fallers and M. J. Levy, Jr., "The Family: Some Comparative Considerations," *American Anthropologist,* Vol. 61, No. 4 (August 1959), pp. 647-651.

[5] The conception of all relationships involving sexual intercourse without orientation to descent as portions of kinship structure does violence to some conventional usage. Professor G. P. Murdock has written me, and I am sure many others would agree, that in the context of societies characterized by less concern for confining sexual intercourse to the marital relationship such intercourse occurs "in a variety of social contexts, many of which relate in no way to kinship structure and family units." To some extent this is purely a matter of definition, but the procedure followed here is not used merely for conceptual neatness. Regardless of the differences among societies as to the institutionalized and non-institutionalized values concerned with sexual intercourse, the probability is extremely high that, either ideally or actually, intentionally or unintentionally, relationships involving sexual intercourse will have implications for descent units, fam-

is conceivable that there could be societies in which all membership units are institutionalized as kinship structures.[6] For reasons speculated on at length below, it is almost certainly not possible to have a society devoid of kinship structures, especially family structures. Certainly the variations in kinds and amounts of proliferation of non-kinship structures as well as of kinship structures is the essence of many fruitful distinctions among societies.

With these introductory remarks and definitions in mind, I should like to divide the speculations here into three parts: I. The ideal-actual distinction as applied to kinship analysis; II. A theoretical basis for the strategic role of the analysis of family structure in the general analysis of societies; and III. Some prospect of actual closure on the apparent problems of extreme variation in family structure.

THE IDEAL-ACTUAL DISTINCTION
AS APPLIED TO KINSHIP ANALYSIS:

I should like to introduce the discussion of the distinction between ideal and actual structures (or patterns) by reference to the distinction between an emphasis on the relational approach to kinship as opposed to the membership unit approach. Rightly or wrongly, I believe the emphasis on the former approach has had much to do with failure to recognize the importance of the ideal-actual distinction in this field.

---

ily units, or both as those are defined here. It is banal to point out that love affairs if long continued, and even casual sexual intercourse, frequently have issue. Such issue always raise the question of descent whether or not attitudes toward such issue are calm and permissive.

[6] See below, pp. 26-28.

Aspects of the Analysis of Family Structure

Briefly recapitulated from earlier presentations,[7] the relational approach to kinship or family analysis takes a given member of the system concerned, designates him (usually as "ego"), and studies the permutations, and combinations of all the various interrelations and their aspects between this individual and all other actors presumed to be related to him on a kinship basis. The membership unit approach focuses attention on systems of action involving a plurality of individuals interrelated, in this case, at least to some extent on the basis of kinship criteria—these systems of action being considered as units or entities for fairly general purposes both by the members of these systems themselves and by members in general of the society in which these systems are found.[8] In the long run, of course, all treatments of these matters involve some combination of both approaches. One cannot, after all, discuss the units concerned without reference to the interrelationships among the members of the units, and equally one cannot set the scope of relationships to be discussed without some reference to the units in terms of which they occur. Until recently the most highly developed of this literature in America seems to have been preoccupied with the relational approach.[9] In the sources mentioned above, I have speculated on

[7] See: M. J. Levy, Jr., *The Family Revolution in Modern China,* Harvard University Press, Cambridge, 1949, pp. 4-5, and *The Structure of Society,* pp. 207-209.

[8] Discussion in detail of why these units are defined as systems of action and not as aggregates of individuals, what is meant here by membership in such units, etc., may be found in *The Structure of Society,* pp. 19-22, 113-127, etc.

[9] As brought out in the remarks of Fallers, this charge cannot be leveled with any justice at the modern work of English anthropologists whose emphasis has been very heavily upon what is here called the membership unit approach.

6

Marion J. Levy, Jr.

the basis of this preoccupation and some of its difficulties. Two difficulties are of greatest concern for this essay. In the first place description, analysis, and the gathering of data on kinship matters in terms of the relational approach tends to give an individualistic bias to the work done. This is likely to be true if only because the questions asked in terms of the relational approach use an individual actor's point of view as the major referent. I suspect that such a general orientation to individualism is realistic for only a few societies. The individual members of most societies in world history think of kinship and family matters in terms of the systems concerned rather than in terms of articulated sets of relationships of individual actors. This in turn contributes to the second and even greater difficulty, namely the tendency to gather and present material on these matters overwhelmingly in ideal rather than actual terms.

At this point it is necessary to elaborate a bit on the concepts, ideal and actual. This distinction is fundamental to all three parts of this essay. By the term *ideal* I mean here a particular way of looking at social phenomena, more specifically a particular subjective view of these matters by some specific set of actors. *Ideal structures* are defined as those structures in terms of which some specific set of actors think action should take place. In the context here the relevant ideal structures are in general those institutionalized for the societies concerned or the segments of them under discussion. These ideal structures, at least in theory can be objectively discovered by a scientific observer. The *actual structures* referred to may be defined as the structures in terms of which action in fact takes place, as discovered (or as in theory could be discovered) by a scientific observer of the action under discussion. This distinction is an ancient and an humble one, both in the general common sense of mankind and in the social sciences. It is so humble that we often tend to overlook the fact that some of our most general and useful theorems arise from applications of these concepts, e.g., 1) there are no people who do not distinguish between ideal and actual structures—regardless of their vocabularies; 2) in no society (or social system) do the ideal and actual structures coincide exactly; 3) some of the major sources of stress and strain characteristic of all societies (or social systems) inhere in the failure of the ideal and actual structures to coincide exactly; 4) some of the possibilities of integration and adjustment characteristic of these units inhere in the failure of the ideal and actual structures to coincide exactly (appearances to the contrary notwithstanding, this is not paradoxical when taken in connection with the preceding generalization); 5) the failure of the ideal and actual structures to coincide exactly for any society (or social system) as a whole is never explicable solely in terms of hypocrisy of the members of the system; and 6) exact coincidence of the two types of structures for any society (and probably for any social system as well) is forever out of the question for two reasons. The knowledge necessary would overload any probable cognitive mechanisms (in this case, those of human actors), and if there were not the cognitive problem stated, the perfect integration of systems of such coincidence would of necessity be highly brittle, leading to fracture of the general system by any change (including biological or geographical change) in the setting of the system concerned which had any implications whatever for actions in terms of the system.

There is, of course, a general tendency for observers of social phenomena to be given answers in ideal rather than actual terms by the members of the societies who sooner or later must be questioned or whose attitudes must be inferred. To ask questions in what is in essence a specially individualistic and unfamiliar form for most societies tends to intensify this problem. As will appear in the third section below, there is some reason to speculate that to a paralyzing degree social scientists and others have tried to deal with the ideal rather than with the actual structures of kinship or with a combination of the two. For example, the family which time and time again has been described as *the traditional Chinese family* was certainly the ideal family of that society, but it was also certainly never the actual family of any except for a small proportion of the members of that society.[10] This latter fact and its implications

[10] Perhaps the earliest clear-cut self-conscious indication of this fact is to be found in F. L. K. Hsu's "The Myth of Chinese Family Size," *American Journal of Sociology,* Vol. 48, No. 5 (March 1943), pp. 555-562. In my own research on the Chinese family system I had only begun to speculate along these lines for theoretical reasons when I came across Professor Hsu's article and the remarks of Professor Olga Lang (*Chinese Family and Society,* Yale University Press, New Haven, 1946) along the same lines. It was not until I sought to check a reference for this footnote that I discovered that in my volume on the Chinese family, Professor Hsu's article was not cited along with Professor Lang's work in the relevant footnote, despite the fact that his work did appear with indication of its use in the bibliography of my volume. This oversight took place more than fifteen years ago, and I am at a loss to account for it. I mention this matter here in a belated attempt to do justice to the help I received from that article. In modern attempts to understand Chinese social structure, it is an article of great importance. Its use in the present connection nearly two decades after it appeared is at least one instance of the fact that its relevance is by no means confined to Chinese materials alone.

when taken in conjunction with the ideal structures have only recently been discussed in either the literature of sinology or the social sciences.

Take another example. Literature of all sorts, technical and otherwise, abounds with descriptions of peoples as polygamous (usually referring to polygyny rather than polyandry) and implying that most if not all males (or females) have plural spouses at any given point of time after achieving maturity. But consider, every little child born into this world alive, though not necessarily either a little Liberal or else a little Conservative, is highly likely to be either a little male or a little female. Their ratio at birth has an order of variation of 103/100 to 107/100. (This is one of the few matters in which race in the biological sense seems to make a difference.) The males are less viable than the females, and as time passes in the life cycle, the ratio approaches 1 even more closely. Under the circumstances, peculiar customs are necessary if polygyny as the term is often taken is to be achieved. Fifty percent or more of males could be slaughtered before or at marital ages, for example. There are other possibilities, but these do not accompany the descriptions. Reference to polygyny is never more than reference to an ideal structure for any society. Only a minority of males—usually a small one—ever achieve it, and they almost certainly constitute an elite by that fact alone in such social contexts. Many further implications could be drawn from this. Few if any of the most fruitful hypotheses about polygamy can be discovered if the distinction between ideal and actual structures is not kept clear.

One may at least speculate that the rich, bewildering and highly relevant variations in the ideal structures of kinship which in fact do characterize human societies have either diverted attention from or frus-

Marion J. Levy, Jr.

trated attempts to generalize about kinship structure and the family in any society. Finally, to close the circle, it may be asked if the great emphasis on the relational approach has not tended to emphasize the range and intrinsic fascinations of these variations without calling adequate attention to the implications of the discrepancies between the ideal and actual states of kinship structure and the family.[11]

On the other hand, much of the sociological literature which has been dominated by the membership unit approach has been overwhelmingly concerned with the details of one interesting but peculiar case of societies in general—relatively modernized society and especially that form characteristic of the United States. This enormous literature has been so little concerned with either analyzing or comparing radically different kinds of societies that it too has failed to bring these questions clearly to the fore. The history of science is not without broad generalizations launched from a restricted base, but the kinship and family structure of this particular restricted case is not likely to be fruitful from that point of view. Intrinsically, the kinship and family structure of mod-

[11] The recent work of William J. Goode, with whom I discussed this paper in an earlier form delivered before a panel on "Sociological and Anthropological Study of Kinship and the Family" at the Annual Meeting (September 1959) of the American Sociological Society, is something of an exception to this. He has made the only general use of this hoary distinction (he tends to use the terms *ideal* and *real*) of which I am aware in recent literature on the family. See his *World Revolution and Family Patterns*, Free Press of Glencoe, New York, 1963. He applies it in his use of available empirical materials on family structures about the world. The descriptive and bibliographic materials he has collected are invaluable to anyone interested in generalizations of the type presented here. Had they been available when this essay was written, it would be longer.

ern United States society is on the whole quite unusual in social history. Even more unusual, however, is the manner in which these structures fit into other parts of the general social structure. The rich anthropological literature which has focussed on the membership unit approach has also failed to generalize. The authors of these works have almost inevitably been concerned with a single society and quite understandably have not been concerned with the possible general implications of the discrepancies between ideal and actual family structures which their works have turned up.[12]

In summation, the following statements may be made. 1) In the analysis of kinship structure in general and family structure in particular, questions about the distinction between the ideal and actual structures have not been systematically raised. The implications of such distinctions when present have not generally been explored. 2) To some extent this failure of exploration may have been a function of the heavy emphasis in much of the literature on the relational approach to kinship structure. 3) Those portions of the literature most dependent upon the membership unit approach have tended to neglect the general relevance of the distinctions between the ideal and actual because of a lack of comparative orientation of the work. A considerable part of this literature has fallen into this state because it is preoccupied with the state of affairs characteristic of one specific society—and preoccupied with that for its intrinsic interest rather than any general comparative relevance.

[12] Examples of this sort will be found in the works cited by Fallers below.

Marion J. Levy, Jr.

A THEORETICAL BASIS FOR THE STRATEGIC ROLE OF THE ANALYSIS OF FAMILY STRUCTURE IN THE GENERAL ANALYSIS OF SOCIETIES

Some of the fascination with kinship in general and the family in particular as a focus for social analysis has been sentimental, some ethical, and a great deal therapeutic. However far the source of concern may have been removed from scientific considerations, the concern itself has hardly been misplaced from the point of view of social science. It is particularly apposite for those interested in highly generalized theory. For many years, through all the vicissitudes of cultural relativity and its opposite, certain propositions on the most general level of analysis have been relatively well accepted and verified. Most obvious is the fact that there is no society known historically or currently in which there is *no* institutionalized family structure. How the family structures are organized, what is done in terms of them, and how they interrelate with other membership units and aspects of the social structure are all subject to extremely wide variation, but the fact of their presence is as certain as the fact of evolution.

Hardly more controversial is another proposition that always furnishes a minimal lead on the interrelations of these and other structures. This is the existence of an incest taboo. There is no known society totally lacking in an incest taboo. Indeed, only relatively rarely, and then for carefully defined and delimited members of the society is some form of the incest taboo held in abeyance ideally. The members involved in such an abeyance never form anything approaching a substantial portion of the members of a society. Usually, if such exemption is present at all, no more than a ruler's kinfolk or a similarly re-

Aspects of the Analysis of Family Structure

stricted category is permitted the exemption. Actual infractions, of course, vary widely in kind and incidence among societies. Not only is the incest taboo always present in some form for the general members of a society as a whole, but the taboo always covers the specific relationships of mother-son, father-daughter, and brother-sister if the individuals so designated are known.[13] Beyond these relationships the institutionalized form of the incest taboo for different societies varies widely. For example, for a strict Confucian gentry family of traditional China, sexual relations between any two individuals of the same surname were interdicted under the incest taboo. As a minimum, the presence of the incest taboo always furnishes leads on the probabilities and possibilities of solidarity structures as sub-systems of any given kinship and/or family units. It also furnishes leads on certain minimal interrelationships between one set of kinship and/or family structures and another. Finally, it usually furnishes leads on certain minimal interrelationships between kinship and/or family structures and certain nonkinship structures if those exist in the society concerned.

For present purposes it is not necessary to tarry over the many lists of functions attributed to the operation of humans in terms of family structures. A careful study of the functional requisites of any family (and/or kinship structure) is not yet in hand. Certainly there is not in hand a careful study of the minimal functions that must be performed in terms

[13] Fathers are not always known in all social contexts. Whenever known, for the members of the society as a whole, the father-daughter relationship is taboo. Similarly, even when the true biological identities of the fathers and daughters are not known, sexual relationships among those socially defined as being in such roles or closely similar roles, whether by adoption or whatnot, are taboo.

14

Marion J. Levy, Jr.

of family (and/or kinship) structure for any society (or of the family and/or kinship structures which must be present) if that society is to survive. This does not exist even as a model (or system of analysis). Suffice it to say that flexibility of family structures, as of other concrete structures, is so great that the functions which result from operation in terms of their systems of action vary enormously. However great this variation may be, some of the institutions present in these systems are always crucial institutions for the society concerned on any level of generalization with regard to that society. Furthermore, despite the fact that there is extremely wide variation in the degree and manner in which different societies may be spoken of as "family oriented" or "kinship oriented" (i.e., the extent to which the members of those societies are institutionally expected by other members of their society to make decisions about alternative behavior on the basis of family or other kinship considerations), the tenability of the preceding statement is not affected. Variations in the degree and kind of family orientation only alter the magnitude and kind of crucial institutions which inhere in these concrete structures, if the societies concerned are to be stable.

Consideration of family structures offers another sort of advantage in the construction of general systems of analysis for societies. Heretofore in constructing systems of analysis for societies on the basis of structural requisites, we have been confined to systems either explicitly or implicitly derived in terms of analytic structural requisites rather than concrete ones. From a theoretical point of view the empirical universality of family structures does not suffice to justify an alternative procedure. In the past we have not been able to answer satisfactorily the question,

Aspects of the Analysis of Family Structure

"Could not the empirical universality of these structures indicate a lack of social inventiveness rather than that they are concrete structural requisites?" Unless there is a sound argument to the effect that no amount of social inventiveness could produce an alternative to family structure, development of a set of concrete structural requisites is in some difficulty. If family structure is not a concrete structural requisite for *any* society, where among concrete structures should one search for a fruitful beginning to the quest for concrete structural requisites of *any* society?

There are many reasons for seeking a set of concrete structural requisites for *any* society. Not the least of these is the extreme difficulty that most of us have in using analytic distinctions without falling into the fallacy of reification. Another is of course the semblance of greater descriptive utility such procedure would give, especially since all social materials are in fact derived by observations of the behavior of actors operating in terms of some specific concrete social structures.

After a long history of struggle to get rid of naïve biological determinism (and a subsequent less vigorous struggle to get away from naive assertions of biological irrelevancy), we are approaching a period of increasingly fruitful cooperation across the disciplinary lines of biology and social science. In some cases a fruitful element of reductionism from one scientific level to another may be at hand.[14] One of these which seems exeedingly likely within a short

[14] For a discussion of reductionism, primitive and retarded, see M. J. Levy, Jr., "Some Problems for a Unified Theory of Human Nature," *Sociological Theory, Values, and Sociocultural Change: Essays in Honor of P. A. Sorokin,* Ed. E. A. Tiryakian, Free Press, Glencoe, 1963, pp. 15-20.

time bears directly on this point. There is increasingly abundant evidence and theorizing to the effect that mature and stable adults of the human species cannot develop without certain types of relationships. The functions of these relationships can by no means be confined to the provision of food, clothing, and shelter. As a minimum they have to do also with certain types of cognitive and affective interaction. In recent years there has been some reason to hold that even certain functions hitherto considered autonomic functions have some basis in such interrelations.[15] In the absence of mystical explanations, all of cognition and (hence probably everything else)[16] is certainly so dependent.

[15] This assertion should be taken with special caution. I have lost the specific source I had in mind here. I thought I had learned of it nearly twenty years ago from Professor Talcott Parsons. He cannot recall the case, however. The case in mind had to do with a very young infant neglected by her (?) parents. The infant arrived in a hospital (I believe in Philadelphia) in a state of serious malnutrition. There she was discovered, by some means, not to secrete gastric juices upon the ingestion of food. This function, generally believed to be autonomic, did not take place until affective attention at feeding was given by a member of the hospital staff.

The reader has a right to be informed as to the vagueness of this basis of the present line of speculation, but it is presented only as a line of speculation. As indicated below for present purposes the non-social biological speculation presented here may be taken not merely as hypotheses but as assumptions on my part. Readers better versed in these matters will probably vary widely in the extent to which they regard available experimental or clinical experience as supporting the assumptions made here.

[16] For speculation on the strategic nature of cognition in such matters see: M. Kochen and M. J. Levy, Jr., "The Logical Nature of an Active Scheme," *Behavioral Science,* Vol. 1, No. 4 (October 1956), pp. 265-289.

Aspects of the Analysis of Family Structure

As in the case of the standing of family structures as concrete structural requisites the question of a lack of social inventiveness may be raised with regard to provision of the "necessary" interaction on a family basis. Can the minimal requirements for cognitive and affective interaction, let alone the provision of food, clothing and shelter, be provided altogether in terms of non-kinship organizations? The fact that to some extent these cognitive and affective interactions in terms of all known societies have taken place in family settings does not settle this issue. It says *only* that these requisite interactions have been so provided to some extent in terms of all known societies. The original claims of the Chinese Communists for their communes and the assertions occasionally met about the kibbutzim cannot be taken as demonstrations in contradiction.[17] Never-

[17] M. E. Spiro ("Is the Family Universal," *American Anthropologist,* Vol. 56, No. 5, Part 1, pp. 839-846) took this line as a professional anthropologist despite the facts that: 1) he did not attempt to establish the kibbutz as a self-sufficient sub-system of Israeli society or as setting the pattern for that society as a whole; 2) he did not demonstrate that a set of stable adults had yet been produced in terms of kibbutz structures (though it may well have been); and 3) he did not even demonstrate that the kibbutz studied had totally eliminated family structures. It is interesting that in a subsequent reprint (*The Family,* ed. by N. W. Bell and E. F. Vogel, Free Press, Glencoe, 1960, pp. 64-75) Professor Spiro modified and amplified his earlier position.

The claims of the Chinese Communists for their communes received wide publicity, but those claims do not have to be taken at face value. The communes, as described in terms of total elimination of the family, almost certainly never went into full effect for a vast proportion of the members of Chinese society under communist control. Recent press reports indicate even official withdrawals from these extreme goals and claims. No one has reason to doubt that the disintegration of the traditional Chinese family was

theless the empirical universality of these interactions in family contexts will never establish them as requisites. In the absence of some theoretical argument to the effect that these interactions must and/or will take place in family contexts if a society is to continue to exist, the importance of these interactions for the development of stable adults cannot be used to establish the family as a concrete structural requisite.

I assume that factors explicable in non-social biological terms will soon prove definitively that the probability of an attempt at some family relationship, however modified socially, is extremely high. I assume that this probability is high enough at least to account for a generally strong emotional bond between mother and infant. I assume that the attempt at some such family relationship will be initiated by the biological mother toward her biological child under ordinary circumstances. I assume that there is a high probability that the relationship so initiated will, for reasons initially explicable in purely biological terms be responded to by the newborn infant. I assume that that response will in some sense reinforce the relationship. I assume that from that point on the relationship becomes an interdependent one with functions not explicable purely in biological terms—given the present state of our knowledge of biology.[18] I assume that the probability of the biological mother being so motivated has to do with physio-

---

greatly further accelerated under communist rule, but that state of affairs is not to be confused with extermination of family systems—or even near extermination of them.

[18] For development of one line of hypothesis about the emergence of differences which may be termed social as distinct from biological from such a relationship see M. Kochen, and M. J. Levy, Jr., *op. cit.*

logical factors such as hormonal balances at time of parturition. From an evolutionary point of view I would expect this sort of "motivation" to precede and/or be essential in explanation of the development of what many today would dub the "cultural" or "social" factors characteristic of these relationships as we know them.

It is not necessary for this line of assumption or hypothesis to assume any mysterious or special sense by which the biological mother is able to recognize her actual biological offspring unerringly or nearly so. It is enough that at the time of parturition the probability be high that she has an opportunity to interact with some newborn infant. If such opportunity exists under most circumstances with many mammalian species the probability would be high that the interaction would in fact be between a biologically related mother and infant. This line of reasoning is in no way refractory to the possibility of substituting foster-mothers for biological mothers in many cases. As will be seen below (pp. 21-24), however, it is assumed that without some involvement of women who have very recently borne children such interaction cannot be systematically enough provided for infants to develop into stable adults.

There are probably many scientists who would assert that the evidence on this score is already overwhelming. Except for an over reaction against biological determinism of a naïve sort there is no cause to find this surprising. Most, if not all, mammalian species other than man display such behavior as also do many non-mammalian species. In the human species, at least, the mother-infant connection is the most obvious place to look for such a probability, but here it should be borne in mind that an apparently biologically determined predisposition of males in some species toward such behavior is by no means rare. This is perhaps particularly obvious with regard to hatching, feeding, and protective behavior. It should go without saying that such a line of speculation in no way asserts that social factors cannot offset such biological probabilities. Both mothers and fathers apathetically or even destructively inclined toward their offspring are well-known amongst humans and among representatives of other species in which sustaining protective behavior is extremely probable.

If the line of assumption (or hypothesis) is to be elegant on the score of family interaction as a functional requisite of any society and hence of a family system as a concrete structural requisite, we shall need still another element, i.e., some indication that although such interaction may be otherwise brought about, the probability that it will in fact be so induced is not sufficiently great to account for the persistence of any society. That is to say such interaction between an infant and some person other than the mother or other kin-folk is either unlikely or if present is not likely to be effective in enough cases to hold the prospect of producing enough stable adults to continue operation in terms of the society concerned. If such an hypothesis were to prove to be empirically tenable, the possibility that the empirical universality of kinship and family units was simply a function of the lack of social inventiveness would be removed. Therefore, in addition to the assumption or hypothesis of high probability that mothers will be motivated to form an affectively oriented relationship with their infants if those are known and available, I would also hypothesize that it is not feasible that similar functions be systematically performed by individuals other than the biological mothers.

Aspects of the Analysis of Family Structure

There is no difficulty in conceiving of such substitutions in an individual case, of course. There is not even any difficulty in conceiving of this as applying to a specific class provided the individuals of that class have access to special means and do not form a large proportion of the members of the society concerned. For reasons too complicated to go into here, this can probably not be true of any save representatives of a class of very considerable prestige and/or power in a society.[19] Such a restricted segment of the membership of a society might do this and still produce stable adults. For example, sufficiently motivated and capable foster mothers or wet nurses might be found. On the other hand, it is even conceivable that the members of such a class not produce stable adults to replace themselves and yet be so integrated into the rest of the social structure that this failure would not have major implications for the stability of the system as a whole.[20]

[19] The Japanese feudal lords, the *daimyo*, were representatives of a class of this sort. Their children were literally reared by retainers, and the role of those retainers was not just that of nurse, even in the sense of the famed English nanny. The *kerai* in charge of these children furnished much of their closest approach to "social" parents. Especially in their early years, their biological parents saw little of them. In later years sons were likely to see something of their actual fathers, but this was no ordinary father-son relationship for Japanese society of that time. The *daimyo* formed an important class, but they were not numerous either absolutely or relative to other segments of the society. It might also be added that we lack personality studies of *daimyo* children grown to adulthood. We know little, therefore, as to whether this putting-out system for children was or was not conducive to developing stable adults. Nor do we know its effects on their mothers.

[20] Again one may speculate about the *daimyo*. They operated in terms of what amounted to a system of "absentee administration" in which the character of the individual

22

Marion J. Levy, Jr.

For the general membership of a society as a whole neither of the two possibilities mentioned just above holds true. In terms of no society has the general membership had the resources to farm out its children to others. Even if the resources were available one might raise a question like that of "who guards the guards themselves?" I.e., "Who nurses the nurses' children"? But there are more fundamental questions which can be raised than that of resources or the nursing of the nurses' children. I would hypothesize as follows. There is a limit on the level of specialization here. In the first place, it is unlikely that one be able systematically to motivate non-mothers to give the relevant kinds of affective and other interactions to infants. In the second place, the ratio of specialists of this sort to charges must be very high—not much less than that consistent with the maximum fertility of women.[21] There is growing evidence, I am told, that with the best intentioned staffs available and with far better sanitary conditions than generally prevail in family settings, orphanages and other such organizations have curiously high death-rates, incidence of disease, and problems of adjustment for the individuals who undergo this sort of rearing. Certainly the leaders of no society have been successful in any attempt to institutionalize such practices for all or most of its members.

---

daimyo did not ordinarily matter very much; theirs was a bureaucratic structure in terms of which no legitimate ruler really administered and no administrator ruled. In fact *daimyo* seem rarely to have dominated their bureaucracies, and the members of their bureaucracies seem rarely to have defied their *daimyo*—or ever wished to do so.

[21] Probably it would not be that low. There are a few notable examples of mothers rearing very large sets of children sucessfully, but in general, infant mortality has been such that this problem was not posed even when fertility was high.

Aspects of the Analysis of Family Structure

If a nurse system of some sort is to be substituted for a family system, if it is important that the nurses themselves be mothers, even though they do not nurse their own children, and if it is important that the ratio of nurses to infants be no smaller than one would ordinarily encounter in the ratio of mothers to infants and small children, then it is, of course, conceivable that there be a system in terms of which somehow each mother nursed another's children roughly of the age of her own. The evolution of such a system of parental musical chairs would, however, contain much more of the improbable and the quixotic than the development of any known family structures.

It would not be necessary to go to any such lengths with regard to the relation between father and infant. Indeed, a reduction to the biological level of that relationship, given information currently at hand, is much less likely for fairly obvious reasons. The mechanisms for this sort of a relationship are far more likely to operate psychologically and socially than in any direct physiological fashion. At the same time one ought not overlook the possibility of physiologically explicable factors as a function of the psychological and social relations between more or less regular sex partners. Again in other parts of the animal world such factors are not infrequent. The hatching behavior of many avian species, for example, is neither mysterious nor social as far as we know. Even in mammalian species the association between a mother-infant pair and some male (usually the regular sex partner of the mother and therefore likely to be the biological father of the infant) is by no means rare. Even if this relationship is more difficult to establish, if the probability is exceedingly high for whatever reasons that the mother and infant

Marion J. Levy, Jr.

will form a unit of solidarity, then it is exceedingly likely, if only for social reasons that some other individual(s) will be associated with that unit and that one of these be a male. If that male is a sex partner of the mother, and that is also likely for social reasons, we have quite enough to establish the necessity of kinship and family structure. Even in the absence of the argument about the male sex partner, the necessity of some kinship unit would be established.[22]

At this point I should like to recapitulate the line of argument briefly and introduce the next step. In the attempt to establish the strategic nature of family structure in the general analysis of social structure three major lines are pursued here. The first two have just been discussed. The third follows immediately. The first more or less speaks for itself and is purely empirical rather than theoretical. This is the fact that there exists no known society which lacks family structure, i.e., as far as we know family structure is empirically universal. This does not say that every individual is reared in a family setting—merely that there are no societies such that no indi-

[22] In the absence of the male partner, this kinship unit would be of type #1, descent units, rather than type #3, family units (see definitions p. 4). They would however be a special case of descent units since the descent elements oriented to by the members would always cluster about one or more mother-infant relationships. If this type of descent unit be considered type #1a and the assumptions made about an associated male sex partner are invalid, then the remaining arguments in this essay would refer to family units and/or units of type #1a. It is the assumption here, however, that regardless of how peripatetic or variable the male sex partner may be and regardless of whether the biological relevance of intercourse for conception is understood, there will be such a male member of the unit. If not, mutatis mutandis, the argument should be modified along lines indicated here.

Aspects of the Analysis of Family Structure

vidual is reared in a family setting. In fact no known society has ever been reported such that the vast majority of members were not reared in a family setting. The second line of argument is theoretical. It holds that family structures must be present *if* the society is to persist, i.e., that the family is a concrete structural requisite of any society. The argument here is partly purely physiological and partly a matter of the implications of having a given kind of unit within a given setting—in this case a human society within the limits set by human heredity and the non-human environment. The steps in this argument are three: a) for physiological reasons it is highly probable that biological mothers will, if given the opportunity, initiate interaction with their biological offspring and that the biological offspring, if given the opportunity, will respond; b) without close cognitive and affective interaction (as well as provisions of food, shelter, clothing, etc.) with adult members of the species, human infants cannot develop into stable adults, and without a reliable production of stable adults a society cannot persist; and c) such interaction with infants cannot systematically be induced except in biological mothers on a sufficient scale to produce enough stable adults and keep a society in operation. The third major line of argument is theoretical and empirical, is purely social, and has two parts: 1) If the family is a concrete structural requisite, then other concrete structures are also requisites and their nature follows at least in part from problems posed by family structures; and 2) even apart from the position of family structure as a concrete structural requisite of any society, family structures in all societies share a special set of characteristics which make family structure a strategic starting

26

point for general social analysis. I go now to this third line of argument.

The line taken above is only one line of speculation along which family structure may be claimed to be a concrete structural requisite of any society. There may be others. If family structure is a concrete structural requisite of any society (and even if it is not, since it does in fact exist in every known society), the road opens rapidly if only because of the various implications of the incest taboo.[23] It may be possible to have a society in which there is no social structure that is not some form of kinship structure, but given the incest taboo there cannot be a society with only a single kinship structure. Furthermore at least one of the kinship structures present must be characterized by structures that are not requisites of *any and all* kinship or family structures. These structures as a minimum would have to do with the regulation of the interrelations between members of two or more kinship and/or family structures. Empirically, of course, this regulatory function whether confined to inter-kin questions or more broadly generalized, frequently becomes a predominant orientation of some of the concrete structures in a society and enables us to distinguish concrete, "governmental," structures with some ease. It is not a matter of chance that

[23] It should not be difficult to establish the incest taboo as a structural requisite if family structures are requisites. See for example, T. Parsons, "The Incest Taboo in Relation to Social Structure and the Socialization of the Child," *The British Journal of Sociology*, Vol. v, No. 2 (June 1954), pp. 101-117 (and my reply, "Some Questions about Parsons' Treatment of the Incest Problem," *The British Journal of Sociology*, Vol. vi, No. 3 [September 1955], pp. 227-285). In any case the incest taboo in some form is also empirically universal.

27

some form of predominantly politically oriented concrete structure (or government) is more generally prevalent in societies (if, indeed, it is not universal) than is any other similarly socially specialized concrete structure. For this reason as a minimum, kinship structure always furnishes a lead to political structure. There are other reasons as well. Predominantly or specially politically oriented structures have in turn, of course, their implications for other concrete structures. There is not space here to pursue the matter, but from this point on the way is open to the establishment of a general set of concrete structural requisites for any society.

The material above touches briefly on some aspects of the relation of family structure to the whole question of a general system for the analysis of societies in terms of structural requisites. Quite apart from that exploration the strategic nature of family structure as a starting point for the analysis of any society can hardly be exaggerated. The fact that societies vary widely as to the place of family structure within the total social structure does not affect the strategic character of family structure from this point of view. Here I must return to the empirical universality of family structure and certain associated universals. Role differentiation on the basis of age (both ideal and actual role differentiation) is a structural requisite of any and all societies. One of the requisite types of age role differentiation is that on the basis of absolute age, i.e., the distinction of such mutually exclusive categories as infants, children, adolescents, adults, and the aged.[24] There may be enormous variation in how this is done, but some of it must be done. However it is done, absolute age role classifications

[24] See M. J. Levy, Jr., *The Structure of Society*, pp. 306-324.

Marion J. Levy, Jr.

must over time cover the normally expected life span
of the individuals who live in terms of the subsystems of the societies concerned. Again, even if the
requisite character of these differentiations is dis-
puted, their empirical ubiquity cannot be. Relative to
absolute age role differentiations family structures
have a unique character among the various institutionalized concrete structures of societies. Of family
structures alone can the following be stated: In all
societies at all times in history, regardless of how
many and varied are the roles an individual may
have in non-kinship structures, he (or she) always is
institutionally expected to have some family oriented
roles during every absolute age role classification
characteristic of the society of which he (or she) is a
member. Due to historical "accidents" affecting given
individuals, this may not in fact hold true of every
individual at every point in time, but no individual is
institutionally exempted from such institutionalized
age roles.[25]

To some extent all of an individual's roles are interrelated. This holds true if only in the obvious sense
that they are the roles of a given individual. In this
sense, if no other, an individual's family roles interrelate to some extent with all other roles the individ-

[25] I have deliberately stated this as an extremely strong
hypothesis. If there is any exception to this hypothesis that
comes readily to mind, it can be said that any such institutionalized exemption marks either the assumption of an extreme ascetic role (e.g., members of monasteries) or a role
in some very unusual and restricted category in the society
concerned. In either case such exemptions can never be generalized to the members of the society as a whole or even to
a major proportion of them if the society is to persist. One
may even doubt whether the most unusual of these roles are
in fact generally institutionalized as exempting the individual from family roles.

ual may have throughout his life history. This holds true regardless of the position of family structure relative to other concrete structures in any given society. It holds true insofar as the individual has some family roles at all stages of his life history. Some of the interrelationships between an individual's family and non-family roles may be rather tenuous ones, of course. Nevertheless, there is no other concrete structure such that one may hypothesize that in *all* societies an individual's roles in the type of concrete structure concerned interrelate with all of his other roles at all stages of his life history. Even if there exist one or more other concrete structures which are present in any and all societies, it will not necessarily follow that the concrete structure(s) concerned will be one(s) in terms of which every individual is normally expected to have some role(s) in that concrete structure(s) during every absolute age classification characteristic of the society.

Fortunately, it is possible to carry speculation further than the minimal tenuous interrelation that in a sense interrelates all phenomena in general and interrelates family structure in particular with all other social structure. Regardless of how the place of family structures in the general structure of any society may vary, some absolute age roles distinguished in family structure are always of great importance for the performance of the individual in terms of his non-family absolute age roles ideally and/or actually. It is beyond the scope of the present paper to go into this matter save by way of the illustrations which follow. Full pursuit of the question is part of the job of a general theoretical monograph on family structure. In all known societies, however, initial social placement of the overwhelming majority of in-

Marion J. Levy, Jr.

dividuals is determined on a family basis. A substantial portion of socialization in general and elementary socialization in particular is so conducted. The most elementary contacts with structures of cognition including such elements as speech, feeding structures etc., are largely in these terms. At all age levels important structures of allocation of goods and services and allocation of power and responsibility (i.e., economic and political structures) are in these terms including the most rudimentary learning about political and economic structures. The list can be extended to recreational, religious, and general role structures as well. In regard to all of these structures initial learning and experience are likely to come to the individual in a family context.

It may be noted further that despite all alleged "loss of function in modernized contexts," the family remains the unit in terms of which virtually all individuals acquire the basic learning on which all else rests. All of us learn to eat, sleep, control bodily functions, speak, walk, etc. in family contexts. No nursery school structures anywhere have yet negated this for the general membership of any society.

As a minimum the family background of the normal individual in all known societies sets an important part of the framework within which the individual can operate in terms of other concrete structures. These other structures may be non-family kinship structures or non-kinship concrete structures. If they are non-kinship concrete structures, they may have highly specialized orientations from an analytic point of view or they may be relatively unspecialized in these orientations.[26] Here I intend to distinguish

[26] It is necessary to clarify what is meant by the orientation of a concrete structure or by speaking of it as "being

between those concrete structures such as modern financial corporations which, ideally speaking at least, are characterized by a membership overwhelmingly oriented to a single major aspect of action and those such as many neighborhood organizations in "traditional" China, which at least ideally speaking, are characterized by a membership more or less indistinguishably concerned with many aspects of action. The former has a highly specialized orientation to the economic aspects of action. The latter while

---

oriented" or "orienting to. . . ." Such expressions are merely less cumbersome ways of indicating that the members of the organization in some respect by virtue of their membership in the organization "are oriented to . . ." or "orient to . . . ," at least ideally speaking. This elaboration is not for the sake of pedantry alone. Careless references to organizations "doing things," "reacting" in various way, or "being acted upon" in certain ways is an especially common form of the pathetic fallacy. It flows from a confusion in the use of the term "actor" to refer to individual actors in the ordinary sense and to refer to organizations or concrete structures such as business firms or states. The former usage refers generally to a set of roles associated with a single biological individual. The latter usage refers to a single role (or a set of roles—roles too are subject to indefinite subdivisions) associated with a set of biological individuals, by virtue of their (his) membership in a given concrete structure. The set of biological individuals involved in discussion of organizations sometimes consists of only one member, but even in this case the meaning of the term "actor" is quite different than in the former case. In the case of the organization the term actor never refers to more than a very limited set of the roles of the set of individuals involved. I do not see how the use of exactly the same term in such diverse meanings can fail to confuse and mislead. See: M. J. Levy, Jr., "A Revision of the Gemeinschaft-Gesellschaft Categories and Some Aspects of the Interdependencies of Minority and Host Systems," *International War* (ed. by Harry Eckstein), Free Press of Glencoe, New York, 1964, pp. 213-211, fn 20.

Marion J. Levy, Jr.

usually oriented to economic aspects is no less oriented to political aspects, solidarity, etc.[27]

[27] This is not intended to imply that the specialized concrete structures are devoid of other orientations. The most overwhelmingly specialized of these organizations have members quite significantly concerned with other orientations even in terms of their roles as members of the specialized unit. The most narrowly defined of business organizations must have carefully designed allocations of power and responsibility (i.e., political structures), etc., but ideally speaking at least these other orientations are largely justified by reference to their relevance to the specialized focus of orientation—in this case to the allocation of goods and services. Organizations of the second type also have members oriented to all of these aspects, but for these organizations there is no presumption, even ideally, that one's membership be determined more by relevance to, say, economic than political or solidarity orientations. Thus it is useful theoretically to speak of a modern business firm as a predominantly economically oriented unit—as a specialized unit in this sense. From this point of view many units such as neighborhood and family units are relatively non-specialized.

The range of variation between those units in which no such specialized orientations can be detected—units in which there is little basis for assuming one of these orientations to take clear-cut precedence over the other—and very highly specialized units is, of course, great and quite significant in handling many problems of analysis. There can be, of course, no such thing as a *completely* specialized unit in this sense. That is to say no unit can exist if ideally and/or actually its members orient solely to one of the analytically distinguished aspects of action.

In the treatment below the term *specialized,* whether applied generally or applied specifically to concrete structures such as "units," "systems," "organizations," etc., will refer to specialization in these orientations rather than specialization with regard to substantive content. Thus a guild organization whose members in fact make only a rare type of Japanese bow is not necessarily highly specialized from this point of view. A "specialized concrete structure" might more accurately be described as a "special analytic structure-oriented concrete structure" but such usage seems unnecessarily cum-

Aspects of the Analysis of Family Structure

Societies vary widely in the range and kinds of specialized concrete structures which form subsystems of the society. No society lacks relatively (or perhaps "completely") non-specialized concrete structures. Some societies, however, have few if any highly specialized concrete structures. A society with no highly specialized concrete structures is at least conceivable. Thus a society with no non-kinship structures is conceivable,[28] and kinship structures are overwhelmingly likely to be relatively (or completely) non-specialized. The range of variation is important because of the following hypothesis: *The less specialized the concrete structure, the more difficult it is to keep the roles of the individual members in the concrete structure from interrelating both ideally and actually with his roles in other concrete structures of which he is a member.* Thus it is easier to minimize the interdependence of the roles of an individual as an employee of American Telephone and Telegraph and as a stockholder in International Business Machines than to minimize the interdependence of the roles of an individual as a member of a Chinese family and as a member of his village "club," if such a thing exists.

Thus some interdependence between family roles and roles in non-family non-specialized structures may be taken for granted. But so may the interdependence between family roles and highly special-

bersome. Any further departure from the usage decided here of the term "specialized" will be specifically noted. If this application of the term is offensive, any symbol may be substituted as long as it is used consistently.

[28] A society consisting of nothing but identical kinship structures is probably not conceivable (see above, pp. 20-21), but all the requisite variations of concrete structure in a society could conceivably be carried out in kinship terms. Such societies may even exist.

ized non-family concrete structures. To reiterate, as a minimum for the normal member of all societies at all times in history the family background sets an important part of the background in terms of which the individual operates in terms of his roles in all other structures. For example, some of the earliest structures of economic and political allocation are inculcated in family settings and carry over to all other settings. The general position of the family in all known societies is so strategic in the socialization process as to influence the behavior of the individual in or out of the family context forever afterwards. Apart even from the significance of the early socialization, however, family structure continues to influence performances in non-family roles even in highly specialized concrete structures. The ability of human actors to insulate one sphere of action from another varies widely and is no doubt remarkable. It is never even close to being complete—however badly understood such a state might be. Affectively speaking, action in family terms is some of the most intense action in which the individual participates. This aspect of family influence alone can hardly fail to affect the performance of the individual in terms of other roles. It may be true that the state of the relations between husband and wife ideally speaking should not affect the performance of the husband in terms of his occupational roles in a large business or government bureaucracy, but the general realistic expectation is that the state of those relations will in fact have some implications for the ideally separated sphere of action.

When specialized non-kinship structures are present, roles in those structures seem universally institutionalized as having some implications for kinship or vice versa. Nepotism is apparently either a "sin" or a "virtue" in such contexts. It is probably never irrelevant. The exceedingly general, if not universal, attitude of the members of very widely varying societies that kinship is relevant in either a positive or negative sense to virtually all concrete structures is surely not a matter of chance. In some of these societies, for example, highly modernized or industrialized societies, the specialization of non-kinship structures is carried very far indeed. With surprising uniformity in these concrete structures, nepotism is institutionalized as sinful. In such cases quite definite efforts are usually made by the members of these concrete structures or by the general membership of the society in which these concrete structures are found to isolate and insulate the activities carried out in terms of these concrete structures from kinship influences in general and family influences in particular. So well accepted does this point of view become by the actors concerned that it is taken for granted that what one does in terms of specialized occupational roles is not a "family matter." Nevertheless the members of these concrete structures and the general membership of the society in which these concrete structures exist and "flourish," as well as social scientists, are acutely sensitive to the unintended but well-recognized functions[29] of what goes on in terms

[29] In general I suspect these are indeed UIR functions rather than latent or manifest ones. The lack of intention may in many cases be a matter of self-deception by the actors concerned but in no ordinary sense is this a "manifest" function. Elsewhere (*The Structure of Society*, pp. 83-88) starting with Merton's valuable suggestions about the "latent-manifest" categories. I have suggested elaborations of the concepts to avoid misleading implications. Those elaborations were merely a beginning. Much more careful further development of the categories as they stand in either Merton's work or my own is called for.

Whether the functions involved are eufunctions, or dys-

of the individual actor's family and/or other kinship settings for the supposedly separated spheres of his behavior.

Thus the relevance of family structure for all other social structures in any and all societies has a probability not even approached by other concrete structures. In all societies the normal individual has family roles at all stages of his absolute age role differentiations even though his absolute age roles may be quite different in family and non-family contexts. This is enough to establish the fact that at all points in the life cycle family matters have some relevance for the normal actor. The argument is carried further by the division of all other concrete structures into non-family kinship structures and non-kinship structures. Since family structure is a special form of kinship structure, what happens in terms of family structure always has some relevance for kinship structure in general.[30] In this particular case since the only non-family kinship structures accent one or the other of the two factors, orientation to biological descent or orientation to sexual intercourse, which are combined in the family, this will also hold true on more specific kinship levels. The various non-kinship concrete structures may be divided into two

---

functions, or not usefully considered either will vary, of course, with the point of view taken (e.g., that of the adjustment of the given concrete structure, some other sub-system of which it is a part, or of the society or societies of which it is a subsystem). That determination need not detain the argument here as long as there is no confusion about the term function inherently implying eufunctionality as it does in most general usage.

[30] There are many other reasons why this is very likely to be the case, but here the implications of the classificatory system alone will carry the point unless the classificatory system can be shown to be inapplicable.

different categories on two different bases. The first basis is that of highly specialized versus relatively nonspecialized. The second basis is that of institutionalizing nepotism as "sinful" or "virtuous."

In the first classification, with regard to the relevance of action in terms of family structure for the operation of non-kinship concrete structures, the hypothesis stated above (p. 34) is the general basis for maintaining that the less specialized the concrete structure the greater is the likelihood that the roles of the individual as a member of that structure will be interrelated with his roles in other concrete structures ideally and/or actually. This certainly applies no less to his family roles than to roles in any other concrete structure.

Highly specialized concrete structures are often characterized by institutionalized prohibitions of nepotism and any other forms of family influence. These prohibitions may constitute extremely important ideal structures, and in many cases the conformity aspects of the institutions may be such that the actual influence of family considerations may be greatly inhibited. Nevertheless, few observers believe that actions within the family context are devoid of implications whether intended or unintended for the actor's behavior in his other roles. Illness in the family, marital disputes, events affecting the children are likely to affect the behavior of the individual in other spheres. In extreme cases it is more or less taken for granted that this will be the case. Indeed, there are elements of contradictory institutionalization.[31]

[31] For example, in a modern business corporation if an executive were informed of a family tragedy and went calmly about his job until the usual "quitting time," such composure

Marion J. Levy, Jr.

The second classification consists of two parts. The first, the concrete structures in terms of which nepotism is considered "sinful," [32] follows the observations just made about relatively highly specialized concrete structures. Even when nepotism ideally speaking is institutionalized as taboo, actors in their roles as members are in fact influenced by various matters which come up in a family context. The actors themselves are frequently if not usually aware of this. Other members of the society and of the concrete structures concerned are also aware of this.

In the non-kinship concrete structures in terms of which nepotism is institutionalized as "virtuous," family influences enter both ideally and actually.

The argument above may labor the whole matter unnecessarily. Its conclusion is simple. Either ideally *or* actually or *both* ideally *and* actually, the effects of events in the family setting of the individual actor always carry over in some respects to his behavior in terms of his roles in other concrete structures either intentionally or unintentionally or both intentionally and unintentionally. The ordinary member of every society always has some family roles at every stage of his life cycle. Therefore, there is no stage of his life cycle in which there is not some carry over of influence from his family roles to his other roles. There is no society lacking family structures of which the above holds true. Finally there is no non-family concrete structure of which the above holds true in any *and* all societies even though there may be such structures in some specific societies.

---

would as a minimum be considered extraordinary and might well be regarded as dangerously pathological.

[32] Nepotism is here used to refer to family and kinship influence in general.

Aspects of the Analysis of Family Structure

For these reasons no other type of concrete social structure in societies assures us of so generally relevant an approach to the complete life cycle of an individual as does family strucure. No other assures us with so much certainty of an approach which will force attention to the significance of action in terms of other concrete structures at any and every particular point in the life cycle of the individual. The great emphasis in the analysis of societies on kinship and family units, however implicit its basis has been, is well justified. Indeed, the time may even have come to go into this whole question systematically and explicitly, not only for its intrinsic interest, but especially for the utility it may have in moving toward a highly generalized system of theory.

SOME PROSPECTS OF ACTUAL CLOSURE ON THE APPARENT PROBLEMS OF EXTREME VARIATION IN FAMILY STRUCTURE

In part I above, the distinction between the relational and the membership unit approach to the analysis of kinship was discussed largely because of its presumed relevance to the lack of emphasis placed on the distinction between ideal and actual structures in connection with kinship structures in general and family structures in particular. Part II above consists of a brief and highly speculative exploration of a general theoretical basis for holding that family structure is not only a significant social structure, which no one seems ever to have doubted, but also that it is and must be an especially strategic social structure for the analysis of any society. The argument proceeds first in physiological terms and then increasingly on a social basis. The conclusion— not surprising considering the nature of the essay—

Marion J. Levy, Jr.

is that family structure is indeed especially strategic for social analysis.

Many scholars with or without agreement on many of the hypotheses above would agree with the conclusion or some more modest version of it. Why then are we not in possession of any very well developed system of analysis, let alone a highly developed system of general theory about family structure in any society? I feel that preoccupation with the ideal structures of kinship in general and the family in particular has led to an important oversight. Apart from the strategic location of family structure in the general social structure of any society there is yet another aspect of family structure which adds further to its utility as a general entree to social analysis. For purposes of presentation here, I should like to phrase this line of argument in as strong a fashion as possible. *The general outlines and nature of the actual family structures have been virtually identical in certain strategic respects[33] in all known societies in*

[33] These strategic respects have to do with the following factors: 1) size of membership, 2) age composition and relationship of the membership through time, 3) composition by sex, 4) generational composition, 5) number of marital pairs, and 6) number of siblings. There are many other elements of family structure to which the argument below does not apply in any sense save in the sense that those elements are significantly interrelated with the factors mentioned above. The considerable uniformity explored here is not at all inconsistent with variations as great as those between matrilineality and patrilineality, matrilocality, and patrilocality, etc. On the other hand, the factors mentioned above are highly relevant to such questions as whether grandfathers rule or men have plural wives, etc. The argument followed here by no means attempts to eliminate all actual variation in respects other than those mentioned. I would maintain, however, that the actual variation which the argument does eliminate is quite considerable, directly and indirectly. See below, pp. 51-54.

Aspects of the Analysis of Family Structure

world history for well over 50 percent of the members of those societies.

This proposition has on the whole been obscured by virtue of the fact that one of the most striking (to social scientists and others) aspects of kinship structure in general and family structure in particular has been the extremely elaborate variations of these structures in their ideal forms. One has only to mention such concepts as matrilineal, patriarchal, neolocal, cross-cousin marriage, extended family, nuclear family, polygamy, etc., to call to mind a host of associated concepts both useful and necessary in the description of these variations. In recent years in some quarters[34] a point similar to the present one in its sum of closure has been aimed at by the assertion that the "nuclear family" is the universal one in all societies. This approach implies that this is correct in both the ideal and actual senses. Elsewhere I have maintained this approach to be an error in fact, inelegant in its use of theoretical models, and misleading or less fruitful than might be the case in its further implications.[35] I am prepared to stand by those opinions, though they in no way impugn the goals sought in such works.

If it were possible without confusing models and the empirical facts or the ideal and actual cases in any society to maintain that the family structure on very general levels is in fact identical for as much as 50 percent or more of the members of any society and a great deal more than 50 percent of all the

[34] E.g., G. P. Murdock, *Social Structure,* Macmillan, New York, 1949; and T. Parsons, "The Incest Taboo in Relation to Social Structure and the Socialization of the Child," *British Journal of Sociology,* Vol. v, No. 2 (June 1954), pp. 101-117.

[35] See M. J. Levy, Jr., "Some Questions About Parsons' Treatment of the Incest Problem," *British Journal of Sociology,* Vol. vi, No. 3 (September 1955), pp. 277-285.

Marion J. Levy, Jr.

members of all societies, the prospects for general theoretical development should be well worth pursuing. If the assertion of the universal application of the nuclear family concept is untenable or misleading, is there another line of speculation to which one might turn? Is there a line of speculation which does not confine remarks to general statements which ignore the obvious variations in both ideal and actual patterns which have taken up so much of the time of anthropologists and sociologists as well as of sensitive observers of all sorts, be they travelers, missionaries, historians or whatever?

Since such a quest must be conducted across the lines of extremely wide variations in social systems, to what data should one turn implicitly by virtue of the concepts chosen? Social data in general are hard to understand with certainty, and any essays across linguistic borders increase these problems for most scholars. Indeed, if enough linguistic borders are crossed, these problems become formidable for any scholar. Despite our great advances in data-gathering on attitudes and the like,[36] the data that form the crudest and firmest base for demography furnish the fewest problems on this score. That is not to say that demographic data are devoid of problems. Any demographer knows better. Still it is easier to feel at home with some reliability among the figures on births, deaths, ages, sex distribution, etc., than al-

[36] It is worthwhile for even the most theoretically oriented scholars to contemplate the state of the social sciences in this regard. With the possible exception of the field of economics there is hardly a cranny of social science which cannot be characterized over the last three decades as having advanced far more in the marshalling and handling of data via precise reliable techniques than in the development of general theory. For critics who find the social sciences "too theoretical" and too preoccupied with theory this is also something to explain.

Aspects of the Analysis of Family Structure

most any others. The possibility of misunderstanding is not eliminated, but on the whole it is easier to communicate accurately about these extremely simple quantitative and qualitative distinctions than almost any others. Given this bias, I have attached the argument here to the simplest demographic data I could envisage.

At first glance the assertion made here about the identity of family structure in all societies seems to be identical with the statement about nuclear families which I have attacked. Unlike the hypothesis that the nuclear family is universal, the argument here does not for a moment imply that the nuclear family is empirically universal in the ideal sense. It also does not imply that actual or fancied biological fathers are necessarily members of any family system either ideally or actually (though it would not deny a high probability that this be the case in both senses). Nor does it imply that either actually or ideally the presence of any member, other than father, mother, and children of a unit whose members live together necessarily involves at least an inter-family situation (as distinguished from an intra-family one) or a relation between a family and a non-family unit. The nuclear family proposition as generally stated implies any or all of these, depending on circumstance and context.[37] The argument here in no

[37] A recent volume, *The Family*, ed. by N. W. Bell and E. F. Vogel, Free Press, Glencoe, 1960, is an interesting example of this point of view. In an introductory statement their position is well stated. As in the case of most of the proponents of this position with the notable exception of Prof. G. P. Murdock the authors here give evidence of deepest familiarity only with family structure in a very limited number of societies most of which fall into the category of modern large scale societies. Indeed, the readings in this volume are

Marion J. Levy, Jr.

way seeks to deny or minimize the degree of suggested variation in the ideal structures of kinship in
general or of the family in particular as the proposition about the nuclear family tends to do. At the
same time the real vulnerability of the argument presented here, cannot be decided without considerable
further development of the problem. For the present
I shall do no more than present the proposition and
the line of argument which lies behind it in the
hopes that either its verification or disproof may be
fruitful for further work.

As the proposition has been stated it applies to *any*
society, but for the development of the argument I
should like to divide all societies in world history into
three categories, regress to the less general level, and
treat the categories one by one. The three categories
are: 1) societies devoid of modern medical technology; 2) societies with highly developed modern medical technologies as part of generally high levels of
"modernization"; and)3 "transitional" societies, i.e.,
societies whose members have imported some modern medical technologies but have not yet achieved

overwhelmingly concentrated on the American case alone.

As the authors of this work define the nuclear family I
believe the Nayar as studied by Kathleen Gough constitute
an empirical exception to their generalizations. Correspondence about this question with Dr. Gough and Dr. Vogel have
reinforced this impression despite the fact that in some of
the correspondence Dr. Vogel seems to prefer to reduce the
definitions of the family to so vague a form that I cannot see
in it much if anything of the concept of a concrete structure
which most scholars have found fruitful. There is some question whether even this attenuation of the nuclear family concept applies to the Nayar as Dr. Gough sees them.

This is not the place to argue this question. I refer to the
volume concerned as the most recent attempt of high caliber
to order this field from the nuclear family point of view.

Aspects of the Analysis of Family Structure

stable high levels of modernization in general respects.

Before discussing these three cases I wish to outline briefly the lines along which the restricted possibility of variations in actual family structure is discussed. In terms of ideal family structures two lines of variation are of special significance here. The first is the number of generations of members which are ideally speaking included in a single family unit. The second is the extent of inclusion ideally speaking of siblings and their spouses and the offspring of such marital arrangements as members of a single family unit. In simplified terms we are faced with the possibilities of vertical variations in terms of generations and horizontal variations in terms of siblings and their spouses. With regard to the horizontal variations a special limit may be noted in the ubiquity of some incest taboos for the general membership of any society. Horizontal proliferation in terms of the siblings of both sexes staying as members of the family unit is ruled out. Proliferation of families without departure of the siblings of either sex would probably involve either systematic brother-sister marriages or some basis, probably a non-kinship one for the sacrifice of some sets of families to others.[38]

---

[38] If no siblings marry out, either siblings must stay single, marry one another, marry family members of older or younger generations, or marry non-family members and make their spouses members of the family. The first possibility would end the family. The second and third violate the incest taboo systematically in more or less bizarre fashion. The fourth possibility can exist only if some family authorities are willing to give up members as spouses to those families whose members never marry out. In the text I have not considered seriously the possibility of sons marrying their mothers, daughters their fathers or siblings marrying the children of one another. These possibilities seem more

46

Marion J. Levy, Jr.

The most complex possibility in terms of these two lines of variation is the type of family which was institutionalized as the ideal family of traditional China, the lineally extended family. Ideally speaking the membership of this family unit involved representatives of as many generations as possible selected in terms of one sex line[39] and as many siblings of one sex as possible plus their spouses and all their non-adult children. Such a family structure institutionalizes maximum proliferation both vertically and horizontally. Consideration of these two axes alone, it should be borne in mind, enables one to generalize about several strategic aspects of any family structure, e.g., generational range, age range, sibling range, sex range, range of spouses (and hence, in the long run, range of parents), and numbers of members. (See above p. 41, fn33.) This type of family structure is the least favorable to the line of speculation pursued here. If a society with this type of ideal family structure cannot vary greatly from other societies with different ideal family structures in the matters mentioned above as some strategic aspects of any family structure, then the generally assumed range of family structure is considerably reduced.

The point of view taken here is that of the proliferation of family membership horizontally and vertically as described above. The ideal structures of the

---

far-fetched for several reasons than brother-sister marriages. If the members of some families in the society systematically give up offspring as spouses whereas others do not, there must be two different types of family structures in the society. One would suspect that this distinction would be oriented to the allocation of power and responsibility or to the allocation of goods and services rather than to kinship considerations as such.

[39] The traditional Chinese family was patrilineal, patriarchal, and patrilocal, ideally speaking.

lineally extended family call for maximum proliferation in both respects. The ideal structures of the nuclear family call for minimal proliferation from this
point of view. The membership of the nuclear family
consists ideally of father, mother, and non-adult
children, if there be children. Such a family structure involves minimal proliferation from this point
of view since ideally speaking it never involves members of more than two generations, never involves
spouses of the younger generation and never involves
children or siblings past the absolute age distinction
of adults. Membership of actual families in a society
in which the nuclear family is institutionalized are
sometimes larger.[40]

The *famille souche,* or stem family described by F.
Le Play is intermediate to these two types. Ideally
speaking the membership of a *famille souche* prolif-
erates vertically along generational lines as does a
lineally extended family but not horizontally along
sibling lines. All siblings, regardless of sex, except
one "marry out" and give up membership in their
family of orientation. One is selected to remain a
member and continue the family line. In a society
with an institutionalized *famille souche* structure
there must always be some nuclear families—
namely the families of procreation of the siblings
who "marry out" of their own family of orientation
and do not "marry into" the family of orientation of
their respective spouses.

The maximum range of variation of actual family
structures in these respects should be that represented by a contrast between societies in which a nuclear family structure be institutionalized and those
in which a lineally extended family structure be in-

[40] Grandparents may remain members of the family; children may continue as members after adulthood, etc.

Marion J. Levy, Jr.

stitutionalized. Societies with institutionalized *famille souche* structures should lie between the two extremes.

The argument followed here may be briefly stated now. In societies of the first type (i.e., societies devoid of modern medical technology) the relative uniformity and magnitude of death rates, etc., is such that despite radical variations in ideal family structures from one society to another, the actual variation in vertical and horizontal proliferation of membership and all that those proliferations affect substantially is much more restricted than preoccupation with the ideal structures has led most of us to believe. In societies of the second type (i.e., societies characterized by highly developed medical technologies as part of generally high levels of modernization), changes have taken place such that there is remarkably little variation in the ideal family structures of different societies. The nuclear family structures are the ideal structures in those societies. There is little to prevent high correlation between the ideal and actual family structures as far as vertical and horizontal proliferation are concerned. In the third case (i.e., "transitional" societies whose members have imported modern medical technologies but have not yet achieved stable high levels of modernization in general respects), there exists the possibility of great ranges of variation. Insofar as the ideal structures calling for extended proliferation vertically and horizontally in excess of the ideal structures of the nuclear family in fact are approximated by the actual structures, however, that approximation carries with it sources of stress and strain which produce changes in the direction of the institutionalization of a family structure characterized by less vertical and horizontal proliferation.

Aspects of the Analysis of Family Structure

Let me turn now to the first case.[41] From a layman's point of view, this means societies characterized by very high death rates. It also means societies characterized by very high infant mortality rates, short life expectancy at birth, high fertility rates, etc. The argument here is hinged on the implications of these conditions for the approximation to the ideal family structures institutionalized for any given society.

In terms of general world history the vast majority of societies distinguished by any definition on any level must fall into the category of societies lacking in modern medical technology. What would the implications of the death rates and fertility rates more or less common to all such societies be? In the first place, there are implications for how many people would survive the birth of their grandchildren, how long they are likely to survive those births, how long and how many grandchildren are likely to survive, and how many siblings of any given generation are likely to survive to maturity. Even if the ideal family structures are the lineally extended ones, these implications would lead to much smaller variation from the state of affairs given a nuclear family ideal than general treatment of kinship and family variations

[41] This category is close to the category of any relatively non-modernized or non-industrialized society as I have defined those elsewhere (see: *The Structure of Society*, Princeton University Press, 1952, pp. 51, 106-107, 132, 396, 441, etc., and "Some Social Obstacles to 'Capital Formation' in 'Underdeveloped Areas,'" *Capital Formation And Economic Growth* [ed. by M. Abramovitz], Universities-National Bureau Committee for Economic Research, Princeton University Press, 1955, pp. 443-450). That category is not used, however, because current advances in medical technology have made possible its importation well in advance, though not independent of other advances, in modernization or industrialization.

Marion J. Levy, Jr.

have led us to expect. Actual construction of the demographic models involved appears to be an interestingly complex matter, but preliminary exploration of simplified considerations leads me to believe that even in the absence of thorough investigation of these models the speculation presented here is worthwhile. Confronted with this question Professor Ansley Coale speculated along the following lines:[42] 1) Given a society consisting only of females, i.e., grandmothers, mothers, daughters, etc.; 2) given a society with an approximately stationary population with birth and death rates of 50/1,000 (values not unreasonable in the absence of modern medical technology); 3) given that all daughters live with their mothers as family members as long as their mothers live; 4) given that all daughters "marry" at age fifteen; 5) given the fact that all daughters orphaned before age fifteen are adopted by a mother of roughly the age of the orphan's actual mother and that the adopted daughter then continues as a member of her foster mother's family as a regular daughter. Under these assumptions the size of membership of the average family would be 75 percent larger than if the assumptions appropriate to an ideal nuclear family unit were made (i.e., a family in terms of which each daughter stayed with her mother until age fifteen and then set up a new family unit and proceeded to have and rear her children as a member of this unit, etc.). This difference is not negligible, implying as it does, that if the average membership of nuclear families were four persons, the given form of "extended" family would have a mean size of seven persons. Nevertheless, even under these strong as-

[42] In the appendix attached to this essay (pp. 64-69), Professor Coale states his speculations more professionally and with much greater precision than I have attempted here.

sumptions about ideal family structure and under these unfavorable postulates of early and universal marriage, a substantial portion of all families—almost certainly in excess of 50 percent would consist of no more than one mother and her daughters, just as in the case of the nuclear family ideal.[43]

Any "smaller" [44] ideal family structure will imply an even greater percentage living as members of such units or smaller ones. Indeed, relatively slight changes in the assumptions originally used produce considerable alterations in the actual tendency toward small units whose members represent no more than two generations. If, for example, the assumption with regard to daughters orphaned prior to age fifteen is changed to the following—"given that all daughters orphaned prior to age fifteen are adopted by mothers roughly the age of their actual mothers, but that at age fifteen these adopted daughters, unlike actual daughters, set up family units separate from those of their foster mothers"—the member-

[43] Professor Coale has also indicated quite relevantly that a majority of young children (up to 6 years) might still spend their formative years in an extended family. Only in the cases in which this was actually the case would the arguments here be weakened, and in any case the arguments would hold for a very substantial proportion of all children even if not for the majority of all children.

[44] The terms "smaller" and "larger" here are used to refer to the number of family members. Of the ideal family structures treated here the nuclear family structure is the smallest, the lineally extended family structure is the largest and the *famille souche* structure is somewhere in between. There is no intention here to imply that size is "everything" or that all significant variations in the family can be comprehended as a function of the number of individuals involved. It, of course, is the contention here that a great deal more can be inferred from the size of family membership and the other factors associated with it than has generally been inferred.

ship of families in the society with the large family ideal would average only 36 percent larger (rather than 75 percent larger) than the families in a similar society with the small family ideal. Assuming again the sort of distribution probably common in family size under such mortality conditions, well over 50 percent of such families would not differ in these respects from what one might have expected with a nuclear family ideal.

If one turns to the modification of assumptions appropriate for the *famille souche* ideal structure, the average size family is only 16 percent larger than in the nuclear family case. This difference is considerably smaller than most discussions would lead one to believe.[45] The vast majority of these families would coincide with nuclear family expectations. The reason for this is quite obvious. In the *famille souche* case all siblings of the sex emphasized who marry save one live as members of nuclear families at least until a grandchild is born. The only family memberships which can exceed nuclear family expectations are those of the *main* family units for which a grandparent(s) survives the birth of a grandchild (or grandchildren). The *famille souche* ideal calls for proliferation beyond that of a nuclear family ideal only vertically.

Obviously a great deal of further work, both in terms of demographic model building and actual empirical research is needed here for the picture to emerge with great clarity. Nevertheless, if the argu-

[45] For example, pre-modern ideal Japanese family structures have generally been of the *famille souche* type. The general impression which one gets from the literature on this score certainly belies the implication that no more than a 16 percent variation from what one would expect had the ideal structure been a nuclear family is involved in size of family membership.

53

ment presented is not seriously in error, enough emerges even at this stage for one to maintain that the general impressions given, however inadvertently, of the implications for the actual size of family membership of variations in ideals of both vertical and horizontal proliferation are seriously misleading.[46]

With regard to the group of societies in world history which fall into our second category the argument is much simpler and less speculative. Some factors, which ones and why need not detain us here, (but see below, pp. 56-60) in all known cases of highly modernized areas with highly developed medical technologies existing over relatively long spans of these developments have operated to change the ideal family structures in the direction of small units considered in terms of both vertical and horizontal proliferations. For whatever reasons these may be, the actual families of the vast majority of the members of these societies vary less from their ideal structures in terms of vertical and horizontal prolif-

[46] This line of argument does not take into account the type of social structure discussed below by Professor Fallers, i.e., the collapsing of a set of previously unrelated units into a new family unit. Professor Fallers discusses reports that this takes place when the memberships of individual family units fall below a socially set standard of some sort. These societies may not be sufficiently numerous to damage seriously the argument pursued here from a purely empirical point of view. The allegations about better than 50 percent of all family units in world history may still hold true, *but* neither the reader nor the author can ignore the fact that this kind of society poses serious theoretical problems for the line of argument pursued here. I am not sure of the extent of the damage from the theoretical point of view, and no immediately satisfactory solution to this problem occurs to me.

eration than do those of societies in our first category. In this case, of course, the main elements at work seem to have to do with changed motivation of the members of the societies concerned, and the uniformity is not enforced *malgré eux* as it were. At any rate for this second category of societies the actual structure of virtually all of the family units in these respects will differ very little from those of better than 50 percent of the units in the first category of societies. This, of course, will raise the proportion still further above the 50 percent level for societies as a whole.

The major problem for this line of argument comes in connection with the third category of societies. The membership of these societies constitutes the major proportion of the current population of the world. Many of the societies in this category have ideal family structures calling for proliferations both horizontally and vertically considerably in excess of the nuclear family ideal. More importantly, for the first time in world history because of the easy exportability of modern medical technology, the members of many if not most of these societies already have at hand the means to offset the major previous obstacles to the attainment of their preferences about vertical and horizontal proliferation of family members. In many cases the increase in average size of family memberships has no doubt already gone far.[47]

[47] *The Demographic Yearbook 1955*, Statistical Office of the United Nations, Department of Economic and Social Affairs reports some figures indicating average family sizes of the magnitude of 9.66 (Singapore, p. 221), 7.74 (Portuguese Guinea, p. 217), and 5.19 (Malay, p. 220). All of these cases show a large number and proportion of large families (ten members or more). In the case of Singapore, 379,480 individuals of a total of 940,824 live in families character-

Aspects of the Analysis of Family Structure

Such increases in family memberships would undoubtedly consist of greater proliferations both vertically and horizontally. Initially, however, the proliferations are almost certainly greater horizontally. The initial dramatic decreases in the death rate have most directly to do with bringing down the rates of infant mortality thereby increasing the surviving siblings per family unit. Not until the process has gone on for some time are its effects noticeable in vertical proliferation. There are now, however, many transitional contexts in which the changes affecting vertical proliferation have had ample time to take effect.

One further line of hypothesis may be ventured here. Paradoxically, perhaps, it may be suggested that the actual closure of the gap between ideal and actual family units may itself be one of the major factors creating pressure for a change in the ideal family type—that change always being in the direction of a smaller ideal unit. There are many lines of exploration of this hypothesis in terms of the general aspects of these societies themselves without other introductions from the outside. Some of these elements inhere in such factors as the problems of maintaining solidarity and stability in units in terms of which the actual numbers and kinds of relationships are greatly proliferated. Others bear on the relation to inheritance structures in societies in terms of which general allocations of resources among family members produce little beyond a subsistence minimum even given much smaller numbers and family units. There are several other lines of speculation too diverse to be explored here.

---

ized by sixteen or more members. In this case the preferences for large families, i.e., the ideal structures certainly seem to be having a major effect.

Aspects of the Analysis of Family Structure

The change of ideal family structures in the direction of the multilineal conjugal unit, if that were not previously institutionalized, has so far been observed in every known case of a society which has changed in the direction of modernization. Explanations are many and varied, but they usually hinge on factors associated as special products of modernization itself. For example, the greater certainty of survival of one's children has been thought to cut down on maximum fertility as the only basis of assuring posterity. The possibility of giving greater material advantages to a smaller number of children—the famous balancing of fewer children by a higher standard of living, investing in heavy consumer's goods rather than progeny, the greater mobility required of specialized occupational roles and its implications for family size, all these are factors cited and relevant.

There is no intent here to denigrate or deny these factors merely to adduce another which is somewhat less obviously a function of modernization. For those societies whose members institutionalize considerable family proliferation both vertically and horizontally, the introduction of modern medical technology for the first time makes a general coincidence of these ideal and actual structures possible. It is the contention here that this is a case in which the failure of ideal and actual structures to coincide made possible certain levels of integration and stability. For example, in China when more than two siblings began to survive to maturity, old inheritance structures could not be maintained. More and more peasant sons were squeezed off the land. Furthermore in these circumstances more and more three generational families did crop up. Larger and larger numbers of siblings had to be reared and controlled. The

Aspects of the Analysis of Family Structure

problem of senility increased, and the problem of the passage of authority from the hands of an older family head to a younger one multiplied.

One could go on into all sorts of subsidiary problems of succession to family leadership. It is enough to suggest that the sheer increase in administrative complexity of handling units with four or five members spread between two generations as opposed to units of ten or twelve members spread among three generations and two or more conjugal pairs is itself a state of affairs which requires special socialization. But that socialization is not in fact present in the old structures, and it certainly is not supplied by the new structures imported from more highly modernized contexts. It is the hypothesis here that much of the stability of the large scale ideal family structures inhered in the fact that those ideal conditions were not in fact approximated much more often than was compatible with special levels of kinship administrative virtuosity. Indeed, even this may be going too far. A good part of Chinese literature is concerned with the difficulties of maintaining stability when the really large family ideal was in fact attained. The family head who could run such an aggregation and keep it stable was regarded as having a special virtuosity.[48] There is no doubt that in traditional China, especially among the gentry, many actual cases of very large families existed. The frequency with which the instability of such units crops up in Chinese literature is probably not merely a function of

[48] This is not to deny the importance of the large family ideal. As in the case of utopian patterns generally, the large family ideal in this and other cases may have furnished a framework in which could be achieved the strength of solidarity necessary for operation in terms of smaller units in the actual institutionalized fashion.

58

Marion J. Levy, Jr.

cynically romantic novelists and writers in general.

These implications would inhere in these systems even if nothing other than modern medical technology were imported in these contexts, with the consequent implications of those importations for increased survival at least in the short run. To be at all realistic, however, one must add that such strictly delimited importations can in fact never be made, and are never made. Other structures of modernization inevitably accompany them. All the histories of these importations have involved elements which subvert the indigenous social structure in other respects as well.[49] Again without going into detail here as to those other respects, they too have carried implications for the breakdown of large ideal family units into smaller actual ones and smaller ideal ones as well. In short the closure of the gap between actual family units and large ideal ones is only possible in a transitional state. That closure itself, along with attendant phenomena, makes closure between large ideal family units and large actual family units transitory. If this is so, a stable closure between ideal and actual vertical and horizontal proliferation of family members seems to be empirically feasible

[49] These include, of course, shifts toward specialized non-familial occupational roles, reduction of the role of senior family members in the socialization of junior family members for adult roles, alternative sources of support on non-familial bases, increased demand for geographical mobility, increased urbanization, etc. I suspect that one of the major implications of all such shifts for subversion of the indigenous social structure lies in the implications of such changes for family structures of control. In most of these societies family control is *the major* form of control for most of the members of the society. Even when it is superseded by other forms of control as in the case of Tokugawa Japan, structures of family control are still exceedingly important ones for most of the members of the society.

Aspects of the Analysis of Family Structure

only if the ideal units are small in terms of vertical and horizontal proliferation.

These three categories of societies cover all possible societies in world history to date if not for all possible time. If there is anything like the degree of uniformity in actual family structures indicated by this line of argument, one major line of development of general analysis of kinship and the family lies in the general analysis on the level of any society of this kind of actual family unit. So far in this essay the role of variations in ideal family structure has been minimized. Stress has been laid on the fact that in terms of family proliferation vertically and horizontally, actual families throughout world history have varied very much less than most of us have assumed. But what of the actual variation of the ideal family structures in societies in world history? They have certainly not been illusory. The ideal family structures of traditional China and Tokugawa Japan, for example, were in fact considerably different. The fact that the actual family units of both societies were more often alike than might have been expected does not alter the fact that the different ideal structures made for important actual differences.

The relevance of the ideal structures may be sought along at least four lines. First, the discrepancy between ideal and actual structures stressed here applies only to those elements and aspects of social structure most directly conditioned by the size and variation of family membership along vertical and horizontal lines, generationally speaking. In all other matters the discrepancy between ideal and actual structures need not be as great as the ones stressed here—though, of course, they may be. For example, the ideal authority structures may vary widely from one society to another and within a

Marion J. Levy, Jr.

given society may approximate the actual structures of authority more or less neatly. Authority structures would be affected to some extent if the line of argument here holds true. For example, only relatively small numbers of individuals rather than large numbers would be involved on the average, and the variation in sex, age, generational position, etc., would be restricted. Variations in economic allocation as among societies could be very great as far as this line of argument is concerned and within a given society many ideal and actual structures of economic allocation might coincide. Indeed, as has been stated above, some of these might coincide, as in the case of traditional Chinese inheritance structures, specifically because the ideals with regard to family size were not achieved. It would carry the argument too far to imply that, other things being equal, all other ideal structures were very likely to coincide with actual ones. Ideal structures in general never coincide with actual structures for a system as a whole. It is, however, quite justifiable to maintain that the arguments adduced here do not militate against these other coincidences, necessarily.

Second, a special caveat; the models set up and calculated by Professor Coale (see pp. 64-69) cover only the size of family memberships. Variation of age composition, sex composition, generational composition, marital spouse pairs, and numbers of siblings would vary differently and less for any given variations in ideal patterns. None of these others, however, is unrelated to the factors which account for the small actual variation in size of family membership. For example, the size of membership and number of generations represented are both reduced by the fact that, regardless of ideal structures, few grandparents in history—before the advent of modern medical technology—long survived the birth of their first grandchild.

Third, despite the discrepancy in ideal and actual structures, the ideal structures may still be highly relevant, in the same sense, as utopian structures. They may set a framework within which operation in terms of other ideal structures may be approximated. Perhaps the most obvious example of this is the extent to which striving for as many children as possible under certain health conditions may be the best available means of ensuring family continuity. The emphasis on the ideal of keeping representatives of as many generations as possible together may reinforce the solidarity of those which do in fact manage to persist, etc.

Fourth, consideration of the ideal structures and the discrepancy between the ideal and actual structures remains vital in any understanding of major elements and aspects of the family structure and general social structure of the societies concerned. Discrepancies between ideal and actual structures are, of course, especially relevant in analyzing certain elements and aspects of stress and strain, as well as certain practical possibilities of integration. Many political revolutions may have a partial explanation in enforced discrepancies between ideal and actual family structures. For example, members of traditional Chinese society took considerable discrepancies for granted, but when peasants found it exceptionally difficult to get wives for their sons, general social turmoil was usually on its way. As has been suggested repeatedly above, at the opposite end of the scale in China lay the maintenance of the actual inheritance structures. For some two thousand years the structure of equal inheritance among sons was highly stable but it could not have survived the survival of the number of sons sought by every father.

The hypothesis, that actual family size, generational composition, etc., varied much less than variations in ideal structures have lead us to believe, may hold out excellent possibilities for the construction of highly generalized theories of family structure. Nevertheless, the discrepancies between ideal and actual structures and the variations in ideal structures from one society to another are strategic elements in understanding the differential adjustments of the members of relatively non-modernized societies to the apparently universal social solvent effects of the introduction of structures of modernization.

The speculations advanced here call for careful consideration of the implications of the possibility that actual variations in family structure in specific but highly relevant respects may not be nearly so great as our preoccupations with ideal structures have led us to believe. They should not be taken as a plea for ignoring any or all of the important implications of the actual variations in ideal structures which have been so carefully and fully observed by conscientious scholars. In science it is the function of speculative theory to raise the prospect of our having our cake and eating it too.

APPENDIX: ESTIMATES OF AVERAGE SIZE OF HOUSEHOLD

ANSLEY J. COALE

IN DETERMINING differences in average size of household among populations characterized by high mortality, but governed by different conventions with regard to sharing a common household, the following assumptions are made:

(1) A birth rate equal to the death rate, at a high value of 50 births and deaths per 1,000 population. These rates imply an expectation of life at birth of 20 years, and an average of some 6.5 live births occurring to each woman who survives to age 45. These values were probably typical of much of Asia—specifically, China, India, Malaya, Taiwan and Burma —prior to the twentieth century. A completed family size of about 6.5 leads to a birth rate of 50 when mortality is high. There is no reason to suppose that fecundity or marital customs were very different in the past from what has been observed in recent decades. The average death rate must have approximated 50/1,000 because with a long-continuing average rate much above or below the birth rate the Asian populations would have disappeared or would now number in the thousands of trillions.

(2) The age-specific mortality rates given by the Model Life Table (with $e_0^\circ = 20$ years) prepared by the Population Branch of the United Nations.[1] This

[1] U. N. Department of Economic and Social Affairs. *Methods for Population Projections by Age and Sex.* Population Studies, Number 25, New York, 1956, pp. 72-81.

table contains an age-pattern of mortality representing the average experience of various areas that have recorded high mortality rates.

(3) The average age at marriage is 15, and the average at childbearing is 30. All women are married. All marriages are assumed to take place at the mean age of marriage, and all births occur at the mean age of childbearing. These assumptions make it possible to make simple calculations, and since the age distributions of childbearing and of marriage are in fact unimodal and not very asymmetric, the mean household sizes we calculate are not much affected by the simplifying assumption that all marriages and births occur at mean ages.

Four sets of rules governing size of household were explored in populations subject to the assumptions just listed with respect to marriages, births, and deaths.

Case I. Every woman becomes married at age 15 and thereupon establishes her own household (the 'nuclear family' household).

Case II. Every woman reaching age 15 becomes married, but continues to live with her own mother (if she survives) or with a foster mother the same age as her mother (if her mother has died). The daughter does not establish her own household until the death of her mother (or foster mother).

Case III. Every woman reaching age 15 becomes married. If her mother is dead, she establishes her own household immediately; otherwise she does so at the time of her mother's death. (*Case III* is the same as *Case II* except that no foster-mother relationship is assumed beyond age 15.)

Case IV. Every woman reaching age 15 becomes married. If her mother is dead, she establishes her

65

Appendix: Estimates of Average Size

own household immediately. If the mother is alive, one sister in each family remains in the mother's household, until the death of the mother.

Calculations. In our calculations we deal with the female population alone, since the rules just outlined make the establishment of a household contingent on events (marriage, death) in female lives. Thus the estimates derived will be average numbers of *females* per household. The average number of persons per household would be approximately double the average number of females. *Mutatis mutandis*, calculations could have been based on the male population.

Our assumptions about birth and death rates imply a *stationary* population, with the age distribution of the life table. This fact makes it easy to calculate average number of females per household in each of the four cases listed above. The procedure is to determine the number of women in the stationary population who in each case would have established their own households. Dividing the total female population by this number yields the average number of females per household.

In *Case I*, every female over 15 has a separate household. Hence the average number of females per household would be T_0/T_{15}.

In *Case II*, a female over 15 would *not* have her own household so long as her mother or foster mother (30 years older) continued to survive. Thus the proportion of women *not* maintaining a separate household would be 1.00 at age 15, l_{50}/l_{45} at age 20, l_{55}/l_{45} at age 25, and in general $(l_{45+x})/l_{45}$ at age $15 + x$.

In *Case III*, the proportion at age 15 *not* maintaining a separate household would be l_{45}/l_{30}—the proportion whose own mothers would have survived to

66

Ansley J. Coale

age 45. Above age 15, this proportion would be $(l_{30+x})/l_{30}$ (at age x, $x \geqq 15$).

In *Case IV*, the proportion at age 15 *not* maintaining a separate household is a little more difficult to calculate. It is assumed that in every family where the mother survives at least to age 45 and where at least one daughter survives to age 15, one daughter remains in the parental household until her death or that of her mother. Any other daughters in a multi-daughter family would establish their own households at age 15. The proportion *not* establishing a separate household at age 15, then, is the product of three factors:

(the proportion of mothers surviving to age 45) $\times$

(the proportion of families having at least one daughter surviving to age 15) $\times$

$$\left(\frac{1}{\text{the average number of daughters at age 15 in families having at least one}} \right)$$

The proportion of mothers surviving to age 45 is l_{45}/l_{30}. The proportion of families having at least one daughter surviving to age 15 is $1 - \alpha$, where $\alpha = (1 - l_{15}/l_0)^{l_0/l_{30}}$. $(1 - l_{15}/l_0)$ is the proportion of girls born who do not survive to age 15. l_0/l_{30} is the average number of girls born per family, thus $(1 - l_{15}/l_0)^{l_0/l_{30}}$ is the proportion of families with *no* girls surviving to age 15, and 1 minus this number is the proportion with at least one surviving. Finally, the average number of daughters at age 15 in families having at least one equals the average number of daughters reaching 15 in *all* families, divided by

67

Appendix: Estimates of Average Size

the proportion having at least one who survives, or $l_{15}/(1-\alpha)l_{30}$. Thus the proportion of girls *not* establishing households at age 15 will be

$$l_{45}/l_{30} \times (1-\alpha)^2\, l_{30}/l_{15}.$$

This is the same proportion as in *Case III*, multiplied by $(1-\alpha)^2\, l_{30}/l_{15}$. This same factor multiplies the proportion of women without a separate household at all ages above 15.

Results: The average size of household in *Case I* (the "nuclear family") would be 1.62 females, or about 3.3 persons. For present purposes, the important point is the *relative* size of households in the various cases explored. The results are given in the following table:

TABLE I. Relative size of household with high mortality, and various conventions determining household formation.

Convention ruling household formation		Size of household, nuclear family equal 100
Case I	Nuclear family: separate household formed at marriage	100
Case II	Separate household formed when mother or foster mother dies	175
Case III	Separate household formed when own mother dies	136
Case IV	Separate household formed at marriage for all but one daughter	116

These assumed forms of "extended families" range in average size from 16 percent to 75 percent larger than the "nuclear family" when mortality rates are very high.

Unfortunately these simple calculations based everywhere on averages do not reveal the frequency distribution of various sizes of household. Also it must be noted how strongly the results in Table 1 depend on the very high mortality assumed. If an expectation of life at birth of 30 years instead of 20 (implying birth and death rates of approximately 33 per thousand instead of 50) were assumed, *Case II* would yield an average household 2.27 rather than 1.75 times as large as the nuclear family.

THE RANGE OF VARIATION IN ACTUAL FAMILY SIZE
A CRITIQUE OF MARION LEVY JR.'S ARGUMENT

LLOYD A. FALLERS

MARION J. LEVY JR.'s essay is very useful as an effort to analyze, much more rigorously than is usually done, the peculiarly strategic place of the family in human society. From the time of Aristotle it has been recognized that the family occupies a special position among social groups; the problem for contemporary social science, as Levy makes clear, is to determine more precisely just why and how this is so—why the family in some form (or forms) is a feature of every human society and the consequences which flow from its ubiquity. Some of the apparent regularities in this area of human life may, indeed, have bio-logical (or bio-psychological) bases. In any event, clearer understanding of these matters would tell us something important about the limits of variability among human societies.

The following few pages of critical comment on Levy's essay are not, however, concerned with these broader problems or with Levy's way of formulating them. With all this I am fundamentally in sympathy. These remarks are rather directed to the last part of the essay, where the author suggests that the average size of the family, as well as its ubiquity, may be a result of factors—in this case demographic ones—which are beyond the influence of socio-cultural vari-

Lloyd A. Fallers

ation. If this were so, it would be fully as important a discovery as Levy says it is. Unfortunately it is not so. The idea that average actual family size responds in some simple and direct way to demography—and hence that, under pre-modern conditions, large domestic groups can never be more than an unreachable ideal for most of a society's members—rests upon fundamental misconceptions about the nature of family and kinship structures, misconceptions which, I shall argue, must be removed if Levy's larger aim of determining the limits of variation in these phenomena is to be realized.

Let us recapitulate the elements of the argument: Levy's conception of the "extended family," which many non-modern societies hold as an ideal but which, he argues, most of their people cannot achieve, tends to assume that "extension" takes place along the lines of biological genealogy. This conception is taken from the ideal family of traditional China, where the desirable unit was one containing the maximum number of generations of patrilineally-related males, including all males in each generation, together with their wives and children. In this case, the household consists of a partilineal lineage, which "imports" wives from other patrilineal lineage households and "exports" daughters to still others, as illustrated in Figure 1.

It should perhaps be noted that in Figure 1 each marrying pair has been given two children, in order to make the model consistent with an assumption of population stability. In the Chinese system, when there are more male children, all will remain in the household after marriage. In the *famille souche* pattern common in peasant Europe, which Levy also discusses, only one child in each generation remains in the household, no matter how many may have

71

Range of Variation in Actual Family Size

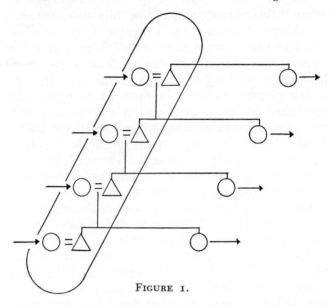

FIGURE I.

been born to the parental couple and reached maturity.[1] In stratified societies, where differential access to resources gives upper class children a greater chance of surviving to child-bearing age, upper-class families may more than reproduce their numbers in each generation, while the lower classes may fail to reproduce themselves. In this case overall population stability and a stable distribution of persons among the classes is maintained by a steady trickle of downward mobility. For the moment, however, let us assume, for purposes of simplification, one son and one daughter reaching maturity for each married pair, for here we are concerned simply with the lines along which "extended family" units are built up

[1] See, for example, George Homans, *English Villagers of the Thirteenth Century*, Harvard University Press, Cambridge, 1941.

72

Lloyd A. Fallers

when they do occur. Later we shall consider the consequences of the fact that in actual societies, even when population is stable, some couples produce no children who live to reproduce, while others produce several.

In the Chinese patrilineal lineage family and in the *famille souche,* illustrated in Figure 1, extended families are built up by aggregating nuclear families which are related patrilineally. This is not, of course, the only possibility. Among the Hopi Indians of southwestern United States and the Akan peoples of Ghana, as well as many others, nuclear families aggregate along the lines of matrilineal descent to produce extended family households.[2] This pattern is illustrated in Figure 2. Here the "core" of the household is a line of females, importing husbands and exporting sons to other matrilineal lineage households.

Finally, aggregation may be accomplished bilaterally, as in some southeast Asian societies.[3] This pattern is illustrated in Figure 3. Sometimes it is the daughter who remains in the household after she marries, sometimes the son, but the result is still a lineally and collaterally (when more than one child remains) extended household.

Now, in all these examples the aggregation of nuclear families to produce extended families involves the maintenance of co-residence into the next generation on the part of members of nuclear families.

[2] Fred Eggan, *Social Organization of the Western Pueblos,* University of Chicago Press, Chicago, 1950; Meyer Fortes, "Time and Social Structure: An Ashanti Case Study," in Meyer Fortes (ed.), *Social Structure: Studies Presented to A. R. Radcliffe-Brown,* Oxford University Press, London, 1949.

[3] J. D. Freeman, "The Iban of Western Borneo," in G. P. Murdock (ed.), *Social Structure in Southeast Asia,* Viking Fund Publications in Anthropology No. 29, 1960.

73

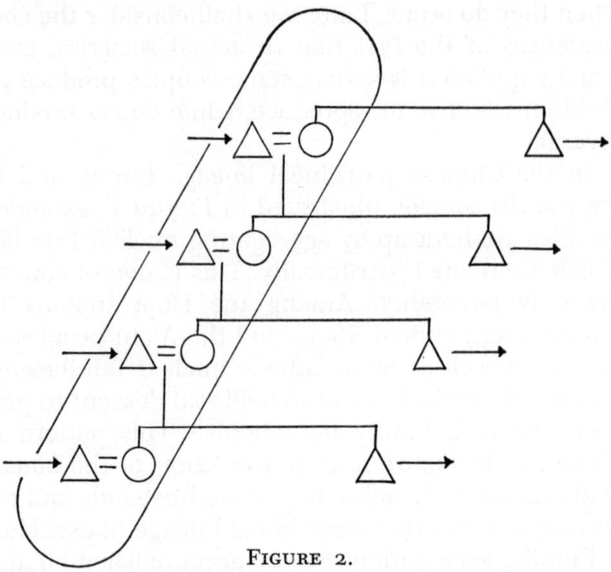

Range of Variation in Actual Family Size

FIGURE 2.

Either sons or daughters remain with their parents. Where extension is collateral, siblings remain together. The lineal principle may be matrilineal, patrilineal or bilateral, but all these cases assume aggregation with the nearest kinsmen. One remains (speaking as a male) with one's own or one's wife's parents, with one's own or one's wife's siblings and their spouses. If further aggregation takes place, nuclear families one degree further removed are added to form a unit containing grandparents, parents, grandchildren, children, uncles, aunts, nephews and nieces and their spouses and children. But in all these cases the household unit is built up on the basis of a widening circle of parent-child and sibling links.

Levy is concerned to point out that, under the demographic conditions obtaining in non-modern societies, aggregation along the lines illustrated in Fig-

Lloyd A. Fallers

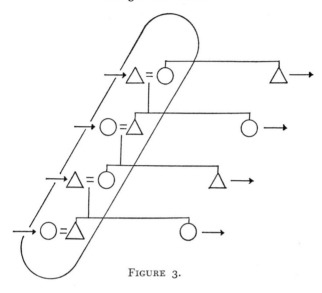

FIGURE 3.

ures 1, 2 and 3 (I have added the matrilineal and bilateral cases, not discussed by Levy, for the sake of completeness, though the same considerations apply to all three), large aggregations cannot be common. Parents will commonly die before their children reach child-bearing age. Few large groups of siblings will survive to maturity. If the society is stratified, upper-class families will be able to achieve the ideal pattern more commonly than lower-class ones, but a majority everywhere must fail to achieve it. The extended family must remain an ideal, not an actual pattern, and Levy has some interesting things to say about the consequences for a society of this fact.

Levy's analysis applies, however, only to cases where the aggregation of nuclear families to form extended ones takes place through ties originating in the nuclear family. It assumes that one will at marriage join the household of one's parents or one's

75

spouse's parents, and that one will not, if one's parents are dead, join the household of some more distant kinsman—or, indeed, of some biologically unrelated person. It assumes that the nuclear family unit is the most solidary one and, consequently, that if a larger unit is to be formed, this will take place only between nuclear families of procreation, some of whose members are also members of a common family of orientation. It assumes a field of kinship relations in which ties become progressively weaker as one moves out concentrically from the nuclear family. In this view, the strength of kinship—for our purposes expressed as readiness to form joint households—declines with actual, biological, genealogical distance. To be sure, the possibility of lineal emphasis is recognized, but within the field of matrilineal or patrilineal kin the "concentric" effect remains. This pattern is, indeed, characteristic of Western kinship systems, as Parsons has shown.[4] Levy's material demonstrates that it is also characteristic of that of China. But it is far from universal, and it is extraordinary, in view of the strictures directed by Levy at anthropologists for their neglect of the "membership unit" approach to kinship and at sociologists for their ethnocentrism, to find him neglecting the possibility of kin-based membership units, including "extended family" households, being organized by means other than the aggregation of successive concentric rings of nuclear families.

In fact, however, we know that social kinship is not always such a direct reflection of biological kinship. There is nothing "natural" about the "concen-

[4] Talcott Parsons, "The Kinship System of the Contemporary United States," *American Anthropologist,* Vol. 45 (1943), pp. 22-38.

Lloyd A. Fallers

tric ring" view of kinship. An anthropologist's genealogical diagram is not a picture of the same "reality" as is illustrated by the geneticist's genealogical diagram. The latter illustrates the flow of genes, the former socially recognized relationships. The fact that these social relationships make use of the idiom of biological relatedness does not mean that they are a direct reflection of the latter. On the contrary, it is extremely common for social genealogies to "violate" the "biological facts"—to "fictionalize," as anthropologists have often put it. When this is the situation, as it often is, Levy's whole argument about the consequences of demography for family size becomes questionable. In the cases illustrated by Figures 1, 2 and 3, the deaths of the senior generations mean smaller households only if the remaining junior generations do not join the households of more distantly related patrilineal or matrilineal kin, or of some biologically unrelated persons. If, on the contrary, they do join such households, and begin to address, and treat, their members as "parents" and "siblings," then, for social purposes, they will still be members of "extended family" households. If a society is willing to "fictionalize" in this way, it is "free," so far as demographic factors are concerned, to have any actual average family size it wishes.

The example is not at all far-fetched, however quaint it may seem to modern Westerners. Phenomena of this kind are extremely common in the recent anthropological literature and they pertain, not to exceptional members of society, but often to the average person. Fictional kinship as a regular feature of society has been recognized and quite well understood at least since the middle of the last century, when Maine and Fustel de Coulanges gave good ac-

77

Range of Variation in Actual Family Size

counts of its operation in the societies of classical antiquity.[5] More recently anthropologists, particularly those working in Africa, have studied such kinship in meticulous detail. Evans-Pritchard, Gluckman, Bohannan and others have documented particular cases, while Fortes has provided a general review.[6] In most of the work referred to, genealogical fiction has been discussed from the point of view of groups larger than the domestic family—usually corporate lineages of the kind which are prominent in African societies. The basic problem, however, has been one similar to that taken up by Levy; to explain how, in spite of the demographic "facts"—the tendency of some lineages to grow and others to decline—these societies are apparently able to maintain permanent systems of lineages of roughly similar size over the generations. The answer, now exceedingly well documented, has been simply that persons are fictionally regrouped to correspond more closely with the ideal system of lineages.

But at least one anthropologist working in Africa —P. H. Gulliver—has, in addition, dealt with these phenomena precisely in connection with Levy's prob-

[5] Sir Henry Maine, *Ancient Law*, Oxford University Press, London, 1931, Chapter v; N. D. Fustel de Coulanges, *The Ancient City*, Doubleday Anchor Books, New York, 1956, Book 2.

[6] E. E. Evans-Pritchard, *Kinship and Marriage Among the Nuer*, Oxford University Press, London, 1951; Max Gluckman, "Kinship and Marriage Among the Lozi of Northern Rhodesia and the Zulu of Natal," in A. R. Radcliffe-Brown and Daryll Forde (eds.), *African Systems of Kinship and Marriage*, Oxford University Press, London, 1950; Laura Bohannan, "Political Aspects of Tiv Social Organization," in John Middleton and David Tait, *Tribes Without Rulers*, Routledge and Kegan Paul, London, 1958; Meyer Fortes, "The Structure of Unilineal Descent Groups," *American Anthropologist*, Vol. 55 (1953), pp. 17-41.

Lloyd A. Fallers

lem of the size of domestic groups. Gulliver reports, in his excellent study of the Jie, a pastoral people of northeast Uganda, that homesteads among that people are, not only ideally, but also actually, "three generation extended families."[7] He says that he at first assumed that, given the high death rates which prevail, this pattern would be exceptional—that with the death of the patriarch the extended family homestead would typically break up into its constituent elementary families. In fact, however, he found extremely few elementary family homesteads. His explanation is that here, as in the lineages referred to above, fictionalization is at work:

> The explanation appears to lie in some sort of compensatory and complimentary process of fusion and reamalgamation— Briefly the theory is, that while there is a continual tendency toward fission in the Family, it seldom reaches its logical conclusion because of the simultaneous process of fusion whereby the various branches of the group are brought into a new balance to maintain the continuum. It will be suggested that such fusion occurs as the result of the forgetting or neglecting of former genealogical links and the fictional forging of new ones to conform to the ideal pattern of the Family as the Jie conceive of it. This process is part conscious and part unconscious. To reduce it to the simplest terms—far simpler than ever appear in actual life—the lineal descendants of a grandfather's brothers are called *kaipopai* . . . a term very like the English "cousin" in its broad classificatory range. In time the actual nature of the genealogical links between such "cousins" is

[7] P. H. Gulliver, *The Family Herds,* Routledge and Kegan Paul, London, 1955, Chapters 3 and 4.

forgotten, partly deliberately; and by a *posteriori* reasoning on all sides men assume them to be closer than they in fact are. It is but a short and easy step for all the men to take the most prominent man of the grandfathers-generation (often the only one at all well remembered) as the founding ancestor of the re-amalgamated group.[8]

Gulliver also found instances in which quite unrelated persons had been fictionally joined to families in this way:

In one case, by reason of long residence in the Family of Longoli, and an especially firm friendship with Longoli, Etuko and his half-brother Nangiro have by now become accepted as established members. For some reason, not now entirely clear, Etuko's father, Lokiru, moved to this family's homestead many years ago, leaving his own settlement and district entirely. Etuko was born in the homestead and has never lived anywhere else. Today he has a wife and children and . . . has a well-established social position. . . . Indeed, it was only through a member of the rival faction in the Family that I learned that strictly accurately he was not even their clansman.[9]

Situations of this kind, where the genealogical "facts" are manipulated in order to achieve a close actual approximation to an ideal family size, are not taken into account by Levy's analysis. It is true that in his demographic model, worked out with Ansley Coale, he assumes adoption as a possibility, but he seems not to admit the likelihood of its being applied

[8] *Ibid.*, p. 106.
[9] *Ibid.*, p. 116.

Lloyd A. Fallers

extensively enough to account for cases like Gulliver's.[10]

We do not know how frequent this kind of extensive fictionalizing to produce large average family sizes is among the societies of the world. A survey of the ethnographic literature might not produce a very definite answer for, while the phenomenon has long been recognized, it has only been studied in detail in contemporary societies during the past twenty years and it is a phenomenon which only detailed field study reveals. By its very nature, fictional kinship often hides its own existence; many of the older accounts describing large average family sizes may involve, not a lack of recognition of the difference between real and ideal patterns, but rather a failure to recognize the processes of fictionalization which make such families possible. But whatever their frequency, the existence of such phenomena in the societies in which they have been clearly documented quite conclusively disproves Levy's hypothesis that "the general outlines and nature of the actual family structure have been virtually identical in certain strategic respects (size; age, sex and generational composition) in all known societies in world history for well over fifty percent of the members of those societies." Since extended families do not always aggregate in the way the model assumes, demographic reductionism of the sort Levy proposes is untenable.

This being the case, one ought to look for the determinants of actual family size, not only in demographic factors (which are, of course, important, given a particular kinship system), but also in the functions which family size performs. Gulliver tells us quite clearly that the extended families of the Jie

[10] In the model, adoption occurs only if the parents die before the child reaches the age of fifteen.

81

are useful for defence in a warlike society and that they form cattle-herding groups of efficient size.[11] Levy has concerned himself largely with peasant societies and it is possible that relatively small families are most efficient in such societies, where agriculture is the principal subsistence activity and where defense is provided by an over-arching political structure. These are, however, preliminary hunches. In stating them, I only mean to stress the point that it is to the functions of family units that we ought to turn our attention in exploring the determinants of their average size.

These remarks have been rather sharply critical of Levy's attempt at demographic reductionism in an area where this seems quite clearly untenable. It should be understood, however, that this is entirely in accord with the spirit of his essay. The great merit of the essay lies precisely in the vigor and clarity with which hypotheses are stated. Levy's arguments have the virtue, all too uncommon in social science, of being stated in sufficiently rigorous form that they may be disproved. They also, even when they are wrong, lead to intellectual progress. For example, though the demographic argument clearly does not account for family size, it does, equally clearly, suggest that where pre-modern societies *do* achieve large average families, this can only be accomplished through the kinds of fictionalizing I have described. This adds something very substantial to our understanding of such phenomena.

[11] *Ibid.*, p. 123.

KINSHIP AND BIOLOGY

DAVID M. SCHNEIDER

PROFESSOR LEVY defines kinship structure as "that portion of the total institutionalized structure of a society that, in addition to other orientations, sometimes equally if not even more important, determines the membership of its units and the nature of the solidarity among its members by orientation to the facts of biological relatedness and/or sexual intercourse."

Except for its careful phrasing, this definition is hardly new. It is the definition the natives of Europe and America now use and have used for at least the past two thousand years. It is the same definition which social scientists now use and have used for the last hundred years or so.

What could possibly be wrong with a definition of such antiquity? What could be wrong with a definition which is so widely held by specialist and layman alike? What could be wrong when the folk-definition and the scientific definition are in such fine agreement (allowing, of course, for the special lucidity of Professor Levy's prose)? Is it possible that the folk theory is scientifically correct? Or could it be that the scientific theory has made no progress in the last hundred years?

Let me start this comment by stipulating certain facts, or what I take to be facts. First, most social scientists do use a definition of kinship similar to that which Professor Levy offers us. The phrasing may differ here and there, but the intent is clear. Second, most cultures in the world about which we know anything have institutions or customs which do, as Professor Levy says, determine the membership of its units ". . . by orientation to the facts of biological relatedness and/or sexual intercourse." Third, there is, or there should be, a set of *analytic* definitions and distinctions which may or may not coincide in some part with the folk categories, or the cultural definitions of a particular society. But the *analytic* definition, however close to the culture's own formulation of the matter, or however different, must be kept sharply separated by the rigor of its use. An analytic definition, as Professor Levy will agree I am sure, is used to help understand the cultural definition, or the folk taxonomy, or the folk theory. Fourth, it is a useful *analytic* definition of kinship which is both the subject of this comment and the object toward which it is aimed. The comment sets out to suggest that Professor Levy is providing us with a definition of kinship which is misleading and useless for analytic purposes, and he would be well advised to mend his theoretical and intellectual ways.

Why does Professor Levy choose to define *religion* in functional terms, but *kinship* in substantive terms? Why define religion as referring ". . . to aspects of action directly oriented to ultimate ends (or goals) . . ." (Levy, *The Structure of Society*, p. 336)? "Ultimate ends" are part of the functional prerequisites of any society, they are not a set of specific, concrete aspects of the world at large. The facts of biological relatedness and/or sexual intercourse, however, are not in themselves parts of the functional prerequisites of any social system, but *are* a set of specific, concrete aspects of the world at large.

The contrast may be put in another way. If one were to define religion as those aspects of action oriented to the supernatural, and kinship as those aspects of action oriented to the facts of biological relatedness and/or sexual intercourse, then both definitions would be at the same level of specificity. Both would be definitions in terms of substantive criteria. Or if religion is defined in terms of its functions—the specification of the system of ultimate values, a condition prerequisite to any society, then kinship can be defined in terms of its functions—whatever they may be. Here again, both definitions would be of the same order.

My point here is quite simple. If kinship is to be defined in terms of its substantive content—the facts of biological relatedness and/or sexual intercourse—then so too should religion, economics, politics and all of the other institutions of society. On the other hand, if kinship is to be defined functionally, then this too should constitute the guiding condition for the definition of other institutions of society—religion, economics, politics and so forth.

The next point follows closely. If religion, for instance, can best be defined in terms of its relationship to a system of ultimate ends, it can best be defined in such terms for two different reasons. The first is that it can be demonstrated—and Levy has done so, following Parsons, Durkheim, and Weber—that some system of ultimate ends is functionally prerequisite to any society and it can be demonstrated how and why a society could not exist without it.

The second reason why religion must be defined in terms of its function and cannot be defined in terms of its specific content—the supernatural—is very simple. There is no supernatural. Ghosts do not exist. Spirits do not in fact make storms, cause winds, bring illness or effect cures. The gods in the heavens do not really make the stars go round, and neither do they decide each man's fate at his birth. Since there are no real ghosts, spirits, gods, and goddesses, it follows logically (as Durkheim showed so clearly) that their real and true nature cannot decisively shape man's beliefs about them or the social institutions which relate to them. Man's beliefs about ghosts and spirits must be wholly formed by man himself. Whatever unity there is to man's beliefs about the supernatural derives, therefore, from the nature of man himself and not from the nature of the supernatural.

Where kinship is concerned the matter seems quite the opposite. In the first place, sexual intercourse can have an objective reality which ghosts cannot. It is subject to direct observation and scientific demonstration. It has discernible consequences —or, it can and often does have discernible consequences—one of the most important of which is that the biological mother and father have a biological relatedness that is, as Levy says so plainly, "a fact." Ghosts cannot really haunt, and neither do the spirits cause illness. But the facts of biological relatedness and/or sexual intercourse have a discernible, demonstrable reality regardless of native belief or disbelief.

In the second place, these two items of objective reality, themselves often related as cause and effect, can be shown—or so it is said—to be functionally prerequisite to any society. Human reproduction is sexual, not asexual. Sexual intercourse is therefore necessary to human reproduction, and therefore the continued existence of any society depends upon it— at least until this old-fashioned method is replaced by some electronic device or other.

It is precisely on these grounds that Malinowski, Fortes, Firth and others have used very much the

86

David M. Schneider

same definition of kinship which Levy does. For Malinowski, "It may be safely laid down that the family, based on marriage, is the only domestic institution of mankind, that is, the only institution the function of which is procreation, the early care and the elementary training of the offspring. Kinship thus always rests on the family and begins within the family" (B. Malinowski, "The Initial Situation of Kinship," *Man*, xxx, No. 17, 1930, 28). "The relation between parents and child—that is, family relations—are based on procreation, on the early physiological cares given by the parents to the child and on the innate emotional attitudes which unite offspring and parents" (*ibid.*, p. 28). For Fortes, "Two 'facts of life' necessarily provide the basis of every family; the fact of sexual intercourse is institutionalized in marriage; the fact of parturition is institutionalized in parenthood" (M. Fortes, "Primitive Kinship," *Scientific American*, Vol. 200, No. 6, 1959, p. 149). While for Firth, "Kinship is fundamentally a reinterpretation in social terms of the facts of procreation and regularized sex union" (R. Firth, *We, the Tikopia*, p. 577).

The issue has now begun to clear. Malinowski, his students and his followers, all rest their case firmly on unquestionable facts. The interested reader should consult Levy (*The Structure of Society*) for a good discussion of why sexual intercourse must be regulated if a society is to exist and maintain itself. Parsons' books (*Social Structure and Personality; The Social System*) are also important for such problems. Just to keep the record of this discussion straight, I explicitly note how important and how useful a job Parsons and Levy have done on such specific matters as the regulation of sexual intercourse, the incest taboo and its relation to sociali-

87

Kinship and Biology

zation, and the special conditions of socialization which are required if it is to be successful.

There has, and the point bears repeating, been a good deal of clear, unexceptional work in specifying just exactly what is prerequisite to what insofar as biological relatedness and/or sexual intercourse is concerned.

But the point of primary significance is this. *There is no matching list of just which particular parts of kinship systems are necessary to meet which prerequisite, why, and how they do this.* For it seems self-evident that there is more to kinship than meets the simple prerequisites of regulating sexual intercourse, socializing the young, caring for the baby. There are aspects of any kinship system that are so remote from such problems as the regulation of sexual intercourse or the socialization of the young that it is just not possible to account for them, or to hold them to be necessary, in such terms.

It is of course just this problem which Malinowski (1930) tried to face with such grand gestures and theatrics as only he was capable of. He tried to argue for the doctrine of "extensions." The family was necessary he said because it was the institutional context within which sexual relations were regulated, socialization and care of the young took place, and so on and so forth. The sentiments and attitudes of the father-child relationship were "extended" in some mysterious way to become the basis on which patrilineal clanship was built. The extension of the mother-child bond became the backbone of matrilineal descent.

It is not necessary to try to show why Malinowski was wrong in such an argument. Even if he were right, the point would still remain. There is much more to kinship than can be explained by the idea of

88

David M. Schneider

"extension." Even if clans can be related to the sentiments and attitudes between parent and child the point remains clear. There is much more to clanship than the sentiments of paternity or maternity, more to the organization of a clan than these sentiments.

This, then, brings me to the next major point of this criticism. It is one thing to say that certain aspects of kinship institutions meet certain prerequisites of any society. It is quite another to say that *therefore* we must define all of kinship in such terms as stipulate the biological aspects of certain of the prerequisites which kinship as an institution meets.

There is no doubt and no question about the fact that sexual relations must be regulated. The question is wheter all of kinship must be defined in terms of sexual intercourse *because* every society must regulate this activity. There is no question whatever that because of sexual relations, sexual reproduction, and hence the biological relatedness of those who are genitor and genitrix to their offspring, that the relations among these must be regulated at least in part so that the very small and very vulnerable child has some chance of survival. But it is a matter of quite another sort to say that therefore kinship must be defined in biological terms. It is one thing to say that given those prerequisites, kinship goes far toward meeting them. To say more, as Levy does, is to say that in some simple-minded sense kinship *is* the way they are met; that its existence and the complexity of its organization, its variations, and its constant elements are defined wholly by the nature of those prerequisites.

The point remains a simple one. There is far more to kinship than the meeting of such prerequisites as have been listed. To pre-judge the essential "nature of kinship" as Malinowski and so many others have done is to fail to see what may well be the more important aspects of kinship.

I opened this discussion with the comparision of the definitions of kinship and religion, commenting that the reality of religion rested in the beliefs about the supernatural, not in the supernatural itself. The reality of the facts of biological relatedness and/or sexual intercourse however, rests on scientifically demonstrable facts, many of which are open to direct observation, but all of which are subject to verification. We have had no such luck with the supernatural, though many keep trying.

The argument is deceptive, however. In each case things seem to be paired, and then compared, which are really comparable. A closer look shows that this is not really so.

If the supernatural is not real, the beliefs of the natives about the supernatural are very real and have a scientifically demonstrable reality. So too the beliefs of the natives about the facts of biological relatedness and/or sexual intercourse have a reality which is scientifically demonstrable. But the beliefs of the natives about biology and sexual relations should not be confused with the scientific facts.

How, then, do we define kinship? With respect to the scientific facts? With respect to the beliefs? If we use natives' beliefs we tend to run afoul of the fact that different natives believe different things, and the shadings and the shadows of belief are wonderfully variable. Though we might persist, as some have done, and say that whatever it may be that the natives believe about biology (or the supernatural)— *that* is the fixed point of reference for the definition.

This problem has another dimension which causes complications. The problem is that the real

David M. Schneider

facts of biological relatedness are very difficult to establish in most cases, and to fail to establish them scientifically is to rest the case of the facts of biological relatedness either on certain assumptions which are themselves shaky, or to make guesses about the probabilities of relatedness. In either case it is not the natives' beliefs about the facts of biology on which the definition of kinship rests at all. It is the observer's beliefs about the scientific facts of biological relatedness. And this, I submit, is nonsense that even Levy should avoid.

A simple example will be interesting and perhaps enlightening from this point of view. The Trobriand father, as everyone knows, is by Trobriand belief not related biologically to his child. Not even the Trobriand father thinks he is biologically related to his child. Or so Malinowski would have us believe. Now by Levy's definition, this is of no direct consequence. Levy knows that the Trobriand father is either the father of his child because he is the genitor, or because he has been sleeping with the mother of the child (remember—the facts of biological relatedness *and/or* sexual intercourse). Most of this knowledge about the behavior of Trobriand fathers—and men and women—is so highly inferential and probabilistic that we are either left with few clear certainties or with nothing at all. The certainties are peculiar, from Levy's point of view, and probably irrelevant, for they are simply that the norms of the situation are that Trobriand men are supposed to sleep with their wives—regardless of whom else they sleep with. Hence it is not the facts of sexual intercourse at all but only the norms or rules guiding it, which makes the matter a matter of kinship. For what is really happening is that the observer hopes that the natives are observing the norms, for if they do, then they will very probably be biologically related—at least some of the time.

Our difficulties have just begun. It is one thing to ask as a question, an empirical question, what aspects of the biological relationship between persons are relevant, and in what way, to their social relationships? It is quite another thing to say—regardless of how this first question is answered—that we must define the social relationship—for analytic purposes as yet unspecified—in biological terms.

To consider the empirical question requires that kinship be defined independently of the real and true facts of biology and/or sexual intercourse. Thus, even if in a particular society a man is considered to be the father of a particular child, it is of the essence of the empirical question that the "fatherhood" of the man be established on grounds other than those of biological relatedness. Otherwise we will commit a tautology. This yields very high correlations, but not very fruitful ones.

So our empirical question becomes this: is everything which the local culture, the natives, define as biological really and truly (i.e. scientifically) biological? Or is it that these two do not always coincide? Or is our empirical question this one: is this network of social relations (however it is defined, but defined it must be) one which does or does not coincide with this network of biological relationships? Where does it coincide? Where does it not coincide? Why in each case?

Do we know just what the empirical relationship is between the network of biological relationships and the network of social relationships we call (however we define it) "kinship"? Is it on the basis of such

David M. Schneider

knowledge that Levy rightly requires that we define kinship in such terms?

Perhaps we have circled back to an earlier point of the discussion. Or perhaps we have circled back now to a point that is related to an earlier point of the discussion, but is not quite the same. Let me see where the discussion leads.

The late Professor Clyde Kluckhohn had a phrase, a favorite with him for a while, which one heard with comforting regularity in his lectures. He used to speak about "the different ways of cutting the pie of experience." One had a firm, sound, and well-grounded sense of being nicely in charge of the problem with this image. One knew very well what a pie was, and one could imagine all sorts of delightful jigsaw forms that might emerge from the different ways in which different peoples of different cultural persuasions might go to work on this pie. One could see, with certain of those who do this sort of work, how a spectrum of wave lengths between certain defined limits of the visible range might be differently classified into different colors. So one understood quite well how what is demonstrably a range of certain wave lengths which Americans call "blue" and "green" are called by just one word by the Navajo. Further, it could be shown that the Navajo are not blind. They do not see those two colors as identical. They can perceive the difference between blue and green, though they put them in the same general class, just as any primitive man can tell you the difference between his own real father and his father's brother, though he classes them both as "father" according to his vocabulary of kin terms. And this despite the fact that not long ago there were among us anthropologists who once argued that because the Navajo failed to use different words for blue and green, he could not see the difference, and because he called his father and his father's brother by the same word he did not know the difference. This, of course, led to the idea that he couldn't really tell the difference because his mother, by the rules of group marriage, must have been sleeping with both his father and father's brother because (and so indeed it worked out!) she called both of them "husband"!

But Kluckhohn's phrase was comforting precisely because you knew just where you stood in understanding and in going about learning how to understand different cultures. One was firmly founded on the facts of nature, and could then see "culture" as a range of variable ways of defining and classing and re-grouping these essential, constant, objective and unalterable facts of nature.

Levy, and his definition, and his model and his chapter are all firmly grounded in just this frame of reference. It is, in Levy's words, ". . . the facts of biological relatedness and/or sexual intercourse . . ." *not* as the native knows them, but as the scientist establishes them to be, that defines kinship for us. There is no supernatural, but there *is* biology and sexual intercourse. It is the very nature of biology and sexual intercourse which in some way is the fundamental material out of which cultural definitions of kinship are formed. Biology and sexual intercourse are the pie of experience; kinship cuts that pie in different ways, but it is *that* pie and no other which is being cut; it is *that* pie and its very nature which pre-determines the possible variants and possible kinds of cuts.

Just as the material the artist uses has a decisive effect on the form his artistic expression takes, so too

94

the nature of the biological material is held to mold the forms which social kinship takes. For that is what Levy believes kinship is. Kinship is the social recognition of biological facts, insofar as those facts can be recognized, and allowing for a certain amount of distortion in perception and recognition.

There is no supernatural, but there is biology. Does it really follow therefore that the reality of biology, the scientific demonstrability of blood-types and genetic relationship constitute a significant *determinant* of kinship? Does it follow that the biological nature of the relationship between the mother and her nursing child is the fixed and immutable cornerstone on which the social definition of the nature of motherhood and of her relationship to her child is founded? Does it mean that because a child will die if it is not fed properly that the role of the mother is socially defined as the woman who feeds her child?

Motherhood is a touchy subject. We have a good deal invested in this relationship, much of it of a gravely emotional nature. Not only as scientists, but also as people. The sacred qualities of motherhood, like the sacred qualities of the supernatural, are seen as attributes of real objects, not as emanations of the human imagination or constructs of the human intellect. The external reality of gods and spirits is what counts, and the best way to kill them is to show that they don't really exist outside the human mind. To break the idols without having them retaliate— that really does them in. For the psychotic to imagine that he had no real father—that does away with him. For the mother to turn out to be an adoptive mother —that breaks the tie and leaves one lost and lonely, unrelated, alienated.

There are thus two distinct aspects to the external reality of biological relatedness and/or sexual inter-

course. The first is the question of just what consequences the biological realities have for social relationships in general, and the ways in which their
cultural nature is defined. It is not immediately self-
evident that *kinship* is the social part of the biological system. It does not follow that because children
have to be fed, that *mothers* will feed them. It may,
as Levy says, be likely. It may even be very probable.
But all the fact that children must be fed means is
that they must be fed. By whom, how, where, and
when are not *by the first fact alone* necessarily specified. And Levy's likelihoods and probabilities are
quite irrelevant to the empirical and substantive
question. The problem is to discover what the nature
of the realities of biological relatedness and/or sexual intercourse really require, and what part of
kinship and what aspects of kinship relate to those
requirements. The problem is *not* to take such relationships as given, or probable, or likely.

The second problem which the reality of the facts
of biological relatedness and/or sexual intercourse
raises is that of how much of that reality is apprehended and in what culturally defined forms. Once
this is known, one might then guess that the problem
of showing how that reality determines social and
cultural relationships might better be solved. For it is
in the form of culturally defined and culturally cate-
gorized and culturally meaningful apprehensions
that the reality has its most decisive influence on the
formation of the cultural definition of a relationship.
Reality cannot exist except that it is invested with
meaning, and that meaning is a subtle and delicately
balanced combination of experience and culturally
defined meaning, and the experience is in turn partly
made up of culturally imbued meanings. The apprehension of reality by a person is an apprehension by

an individual who has learned how to see reality, who has learned the classes that different kinds of reality fall into.

There are certain extreme and limiting cases which make what I have said academic indeed. A sufficient dose of some lethal poison—radioactive fallout perhaps—has consequences which no amount of cultural definition can dispell. A grave wound which proves mortal can be understood and interpreted by others, but not by the victim himself, in such a way that the experience may be a source of innovation and change. But if the victim does not learn from the experience, those who do learn from the experience do so by considering the meaning of the event, and the meaning of the event is the meaning which is culturally ascribed and intellectually and emotionally manipulated by the persons involved.

The reality of biology and/or sexual intercourse, then, does not have a single, simple, universal value which consists wholly and only in what can be scientifically established for it. It has a value in part related to its inherent qualities, but in part also fixed on what and on how it is culturally defined as meaningful, and on what part of all that is apprehended. The notion of a pure, pristine state of biological relationships "out there in reality" which is the same for all mankind is sheer nonsense.

Try as I will, however, even I cannot make biology and sexual intercourse go away. They are not only out there in nature, they are also out there in kinship systems, although not in the same way in all of them. In fact, in different ways in many of them. But there is not a kinship system known to man that does not get involved in one way or another with some biology and sexual intercourse. Does this fact derive from the fact that biology and sexual intercourse are real, and are really out there in nature? Of course not. No more than the fact that there is hardly a religious system known to man without some supernatural. Religious systems always have supernaturals in and around them, though often in different ways. But this hardly proves that there is something real, something out there at large in nature, of a real, supernatural order.

These two peculiar facts seem to warrant some explanation. What is the significance of this? I have dismissed the idea that the ubiquity of either biology in kinship or supernaturals in religion is a simple function of the fact that both have real, existential quality. But perhaps I have been the first to do so. Most of my friends and colleagues, like Professor Levy, have the profoundest reverence for reality, for facts out there in nature. And like Professor Levy, they attribute weight and gravity and significance to what is in nature, to what is universal, far beyond the call of reason. But I have remarked on this fact before.

The problem now is to reiterate the simple parallel of facts; all known kinship systems use biological relationship and/or sexual intercourse somewhere and somehow in the cultural specification of what kinship is. All known religious systems use supernatural figures somehow and somewhere in the cultural specification of what religion is. Of what significance is this to us? How does it help us to understand what kinship is and how it should be defined?

But I have gone far enough. I have set out to raise enough questions so that the definition of kinship in the terms Professor Levy proposes can be seen as highly problematic. Some more elegant rationale than Levy provides is needed. It is not enough to say

David M. Schneider

". . . the facts of biological relatedness and/or sexual intercourse. . . ." One has to distinguish the true biological facts from the beliefs about them held by a society. One has to have some simple but effective system for discovering what the biological facts really are, and not just guessing that because a man and woman are married they are likely to have sexual intercourse and hence likely to conceive and hence are likely to be both social and biological parents of at least some of the children born to the woman.

One has to know why such a definition is employed—to what analytic end. If the analytic end or the analytic aim is to find out how the facts of biological relatedness and/or sexual intercourse are related to the cultural definition of kinship, then it is mandatory that the two variables be defined independently. Otherwise there is a tautology which is not very useful. If the assumption is that kinship is the way in which certain functional prerequisites are met, then this assumption might well be examined with care rather than taken on its face value. For there is much good evidence that there is far more to kinship than the incomplete and badly developed list of prerequisites seem to require. And if the assumption is that since kinship is merely the social recognition and misapprehension of biological facts, then that assumption ought to be discarded since it is ridiculous. It is silly in part because the mere existence of a network of biological ties means nothing for the network of kinsmen by itself. It might well prove to have more meaning for the nature of religious or economic relationships than for kinship. The whole idea that the nature of nature is a concrete universe which social and cultural systems re-define into slightly different shapes is silly. The whole idea that it is the

nature of the various wave lengths which are classed
and re-classed as colors by different cultures is silly.
Finally, I noted that once we ceased distinguishing
religion (where the supernatural is not real) from
kinship (where the biology is as real as real can be),
we might well raise the nice question of why there is
a bit of supernatural in all religious systems, and
why there is some biology and sexual intercourse in
all kinship systems. These cannot both be because of
the real nature of the supernatural, biology, and sexual intercourse. But on this question I must beg off.
This is a subject for another paper, at another time
and place.

I set out to reform and perhaps improve Professor
Levy's way of thinking about kinship. If I have done
no more than shake some of his self-confidence in
the nature of biology I will be more than satisfied—I
will be downright gratified! The purpose of this comment is to raise sufficient question about the nature and usefulness of Professor Levy's definition of
kinship so that it can reasonably be considered an
open question. My brief and highly condensed argument is presented, however, after a careful reading of a series of papers on this subject. The reader
may wish to refer to them. I did not feel that it would
be either useful or necessary to summarize their content here, or to footnote specific points as they arose.
These papers, in the order in which they appeared in
print, are: E. Gellner, "Ideal Language and Kinship
Structure," *Philosophy of Science*, 24 (1957), pp.
235-43; R. Needham, "Descent Systems and Ideal
Language," *Philosophy of Science*, 27 (1960), pp. 96-
101; E. Gellner, "The Concept of Kinship," *Philosophy of Science*, 27 (1960), pp. 187-204; J. A.
Barnes, "Physical and Social Kinship," *Philosophy
of Science*, 28 (1961), pp. 296-99; E. Gellner, "Na-

David M. Schneider

ture and Society in Social Anthropology," *Philosophy of Science*, 30 (1963) pp. 236-51; and finally, J. A. Barnes, "Physical and Social Facts in Anthropology," *Philosophy of Science*, 31 (1964), pp. 294-297; J. H. M. Beattie, "Kinship and Social Anthropology," *Man*, #130, 1964. My own view of the nature of kinship, along with a tentative definition, can be found in my article, "Kinship," in the *Encyclopedia Hebraica*, Vol. 18 (in press). A brief paper of mine which develops other aspects of this argument is "The Nature of Kinship," *Man*, #217, 1964.

THE BIOPSYCHOSOCIALITY
OF THE FAMILY

SILVAN S. TOMKINS*

THIS COMMENTARY is addressed to Levy's propositions that "family structure is empirically universal,"
that "family structures *must* be present *if* society is
to persist," and to the three arguments for the latter:
"a) for physiological reasons biological mothers will,
if given the opportunity, initiate interaction with
their biological offspring with very high probability
and the biological offspring, if given the opportunity,
will respond with a very high probability; b) without
close cognitive and affective interaction (as well as
provision of food, shelter, clothing, etc.) with adult
members of the species, human infants cannot develop into stable adults and without a reliable production of stable adults a society cannot persist; and
c) such interaction with infants cannot systematically be induced except in biological mothers on a
sufficient scale to produce enough stable adults and
keep a society in operation." In summary, the first
two propositions argue that the family *is* universal
and that it *had* to be so. It had to be so, because
mothers and babies are *in fact* drawn to each other,
because human development *requires* it, and it *can*
happen on sufficient scale *only* with biological
mothers. It is evident that both the major propositions and the arguments for them are contrapuntal
with respect to existence and necessity.**

* This work was supported in whole by a Public Health
Research Career Award from the National Institute of Mental Health, 1-K6-MH-23, 797-01.

** I do not mean that the argument is a purely teleological
one. Levy does not argue that the family and human development were foreordained because society required them.

Silvan S. Tomkins

Levy has stated these propositions in two forms. First he defends a hyperbolic idealized proposition, in the tradition of Newton's Laws of Motion, of the frictionless plane, etc. on the empirical side, and on the formal side, in the manner of the logician and mathematician generating necessary consequences given an initial set of assumptions. Thus, "In the past we have not been able to answer satisfactorily the question . . . could not the empirical universality of these structures indicate a lack of social inventiveness rather than that they are concrete structural requisites? Unless there is a sound argument to the effect that no amount of social inventiveness could produce an alternative to family structure, development of a set of concrete structural requisites is in some difficulty." Again at another point in the argument "If such an assumption were to prove to be empirically tenable, the possibility that the empirical universality of kinship and family units was simply a function of the lack of social inventiveness would be removed forever." The second line of argument is more probabilistic: "I assume that factors explicable in non-social biological terms will soon prove definitively that the *probability* of an attempt at some family relationship, however modified socially, is extremely high. I assume that this *probability* is high enough at least to account for a generally strong emotional bond as between mother and infant. . . . I assume that there is a very high *probability* that the relationship so initiated will, for reasons initially explicable in purely biological terms be responded to by the newborn infant. . . . I assume that the *probability* of the biological mother being so motivated has to do with physiological factors such as hormonal balances at time of parturition. . . . It is not necessary for this line of assumption or hypothesis to

The Biopsychosociality of the Family

assume any mysterious or special sense by which the biological mother is able to recognize her actual biological offspring unerringly or nearly so. It is enough that at the time of parturition the *probability* be high that she has an opportunity to interact with some newborn infant. If such opportunity exists under most circumstances with many mammalian species the *probability* would be high that the interaction would in fact be between a biologically related mother and infant. . . . Both mothers and fathers apathetically or even destructively inclined toward their offspring are well known amongst humans and amongst other species in which sustaining protective behavior is extremely *probable*. If the line of assumption (or hypothesis) is to be elegant on the score of family interaction as a functional requisite of any society and hence of a family system as a concrete structural requisite, we shall need still another element, i.e., some indication that although such interaction may be otherwise brought about, the *probability* that it will in fact be so induced is not sufficiently great to account for the persistence of any society." (Italics mine.)

On the one hand Levy insists that empirical universality does not argue for necessity, but he also argues that if his assumptions prove "empirically tenable" then certain alternative possibilities (such as lack of social inventiveness) "would be removed forever." He then proceeds to affirm the high probability of his assumptions and of the assumptions behind these assumptions. We take it as an axiom of modern thought that the causality postulate is an assumption, capable of neither proof nor disproof, and that empirical frequency or probability can never be equated with necessity. Since Hume, at least, it has been assumed that the rising of the sun in the east can never be entirely taken for granted tomorrow morning. The distinction between formal, logical necessity and empirical probability has, in modern times, been assumed to be a strict one. This is not to deny that the assumption of idealized empirical models in science (as in the case of the frictionless plane) may be both legitimate and fruitful. But Levy argues back and forth between the domains of necessity and probability as though one could indeed generate necessity out of a set of highly probable states.

We will address ourselves to those propositions of Levy's which rest on the assumption of high probability rather than on the assumption of necessity. We do this in part because he rests most of his case on several assumptions of highly probable contingencies, but primarily because no other kind of case *can* be made in an empirical science. There is no limit on what one may assume as to the characteristics of an idealized model, but there are always probability values to the evidence which can be adduced to support any model. More specifically, we reject as entirely indefensible his statements of the form "would be removed forever," "no amount of social inventiveness could produce an alternative to family structure." It is more than enough to demonstrate that the sun so often sets in the west and why this is so, without requiring that any alternative is forever excluded as a possibility.

These strictures should not be interpreted to mean that we are prejudiced against model building per se, or against Levy's model in particular. Indeed, we are prejudiced, if at all, in favor of models and model builders. We conceive the scientific enterprise as one in which there is cumulative improvement in the model of a domain through the mutual clarification of model by data, and data by model. Our stricture is

The Biopsychosociality of the Family

limited to Levy's apparent equation of determinism and theory, with an "impossibility" of alternatives. It is rather just *because* a domain is determinate and governed by causality that the invention of alternatives (as e.g., in technology) is always possible. A theorist a few hundred years ago who argued as Levy now does might have supposed man to be necessarily and forever a terrestial animal because the power of the gravitational field made it extremely improbable that he could ever free himself of these constraints.

So much for the a priori, a posteriori aspects of the arguments. Let us now consider the persuasiveness of the *set* of arguments offered. First, Levy himself has told us that the two major arguments are essentially independent, i.e., the fact of the empirical universality of the family does not in and of itself exclude other possibilities. The fact that there are no societies in which no individual is reared in a family setting is itself an important generalization, but it does not entail the consequence that "family structures must be present if the society is to persist." This, as Levy maintains, is a theoretical assumption, for which he offers three supporting arguments. The relationship between the two major arguments is however, complex. Consider that although the universality of the family cannot be offered as proof of its necessity as a concrete structural requisite, it nonetheless is some kind of evidence, for if no society reared any individual in a family setting, the argument for the importance of the family would be completely undermined. At the very least, then, the widespread empirical distribution of the family does not discourage entertaining the kind of theoretical assumption Levy wishes to make. I cannot completely escape the suspicion that both Levy and his readers will be somewhat biased in favor of the ne-

Silvan S. Tomkins

cessity (and/or high probability) of the family, because of the subtle power of primacy and squatters' rights. In Levy's defense, however, it should be noted that he explicitly excludes the first argument as a ground for believing the second. The dyspeptic critic might ask why the first argument was offered if it cannot be used. The answer, I think, is that were this not the case, the second argument would be legless, and like evidence gained by wire tapping, is somewhat presumptive even though illegal.

Before we leave the first argument entirely, to scrutinize in detail the major (second) argument upon which Levy rests his case, let us examine the sense in which the family is in fact "universal." It is as first stated a rather weak and ambiguous universality which is claimed—"merely that there are no societies in which no individual is reared in a family setting." It would be consistent with this statement if there were no more than one only child with his mother and family in each society in the world. But if each society had, in fact, no more than a single one child family, the family would be an oddity among social institutions not unlike Siamese twins in the biological domain. In the very next sentence this deficiency is remedied: "In fact no known society has ever been reported in which the vast majority of individuals were not reared in a family setting." It is beyond my competence to assess the validity of this generalization, but if it is true as appears to me to be the case, then it is far from a trivial phenomenon. Indeed another social theorist might well have taken this as the primary datum upon which to construct a model which might account for a phenomenon of such generality. Levy has used the phenomenon as a base for the construction of a model which would account for why the phenomenon is inevitable—why

107

The Biopsychosociality of the Family

"family structures must be present if the society is to persist."

The model might have been constructed with the more modest, but nonetheless significant aim of showing how the family *has* been generated in all societies up to this point in history. Such a model would have left open two important alternatives. First, it would have examined the possibility that had historical conditions been otherwise the generality of the family would have been either increased or decreased. Such a model would have ordered the differences in percentage of individuals reared in and out of the family setting as a function of critical variables in the model. Indeed there is the beginning of such a theory in Levy's treatment of the Japanese *daimyo,* whose children were reared by retainers. In this case Levy asserts, "There is not even any difficulty in conceiving of this as applying to a specific class provided the individuals of that class have access to special means and do not form a large proportion of the society concerned . . . this can probably not be true of any save a class of very considerable prestige and/or power in a society."

The second alternative that such a more limited model might have left open, would have been the future conditions under which the family would have grown or diminished (relative to alternative child rearing institutions) in different societies.

We are not urging that Levy should have been more modest, or that middle level theory is better than very general theory, but rather we are exposing some alternatives which Levy did not elect to pursue, in order to illuminate more fully the significance of the generality of the model he has constructed.

Let us turn now to the major second argument—"family structures must be present if the society is to

Silvan S. Tomkins

persist." The three arguments presented in support of this proposition, taken as an aggregate, are biopsychosocial in nature. By this we mean that three ordinarily considered distinct domains—the biological, the psychological, and the social, are here presented as tightly interdependent. It should be noted that the major argument itself is a purely social one (that family structures must be present if the society is to persist) and, as such beyond my competence to evaluate. It is the three arguments in support of this proposition which I will evaluate. These three arguments, like the two major ones, attempt a marriage between fact and necessity. We will treat necessity, as Levy himself does, as a fact of high but not perfect probability, so that all three arguments may be examined as empirical problems.

Let us first examine the relationships between these three arguments. It is evident that these arguments do not all have to be true to affirm the major argument. It could be the case (let us call it alternative 1) that family structures have to be present if society is to persist, but that biological mothers are not attracted to their babies and babies are not drawn to their biological mothers; that human infants might develop into stable adults without close cognitive and affective interaction with adult members of the species (or that society could persist with unstable adults); and that close cognitive and affective interaction could be systematically induced without reliance on biological mothers. In such a case children might be taken from their biological mothers at an early age, reared at first by adult mother surrogates, with the help of older children (who had also been reared in the same way) with an increasing reliance on interaction with peers as they grew older. In other words there would be a restriction of interaction with adults to a very early period in which one (non-biological) mother directed several older children to care for a large group of infants who in turn would be encouraged to interact with each other. In such an alternative many biological mothers would be unemployed (as mothers); those who were used might be those who were most "maternal" towards any and all children (possibly including some of their own). The major burden of socialization would fall upon older children. The ratio of older to younger child might be sufficiently favorable to guarantee close cognitive and affective interaction. As soon as possible however, young children would be encouraged to interact with each other to provide close cognitive and affective interaction. Whether the resultant groups, composed of surrogate mother, older children and younger children would constitute a family in Levy's sense I am not sure. If one were to add a surrogate father to it, it might be more familial.

Let us now consider a more severe alternative (1a). In such a case the child would be reared by a few surrogate mothers (and possibly also fathers, with an unfavorable ratio of mothers and fathers to children, as in an orphanage). Close personal cognitive and affective interaction between adults and infants might be severely restricted. There would, however, be encouragement of early peer interaction. The group might still constitute a family. It might not produce "stable" adults. They might be underdeveloped, and somewhat cold and suspicious human beings, but they might nonetheless be able to maintain a viable if rather primitive society.

There is still another alternative (1b) which would be midway between 1 and 1a, in which the restriction on adult interaction might be tempered by

closed circuit TV mutual viewing between surrogate parents and infants, and by the use of prere-
corded TV tapes in teaching machines.

Further, two of any three of these arguments
might be untrue, but not all three. Thus (alternative
2), it might be the case that biological attraction between mother and child is untrue, that close interaction between adults and infants is in fact unneces-
sary for human development, but that such close
interaction could only be induced between biological
mothers and their infants. If it were *believed* to be
necessary for human development and social welfare
that biological mothers care for their children, then
in the absence of a strong biological attraction and in
the absence of a necessity *in fact* of intimate mothering, it might yet be the case that social sanctions
could and would be brought to bear with sufficient
force *only* in the case of the biological mother with
her infant.

There are two other theoretical alternatives, in
which two of the three arguments are denied which
seem more difficult to defend. Consider alternative
2a, in which there is a strong biological attraction
between mother and child, it is not necessary for human development to have close interaction (independent of the belief of the society), but it is believed
to be necessary. Given a strong biological attraction
plus a belief in the importance of close interaction
between adult and infant for human development
(whether or not this is in fact true), it is highly unlikely that social sanctions could ever have been developed which would have produced an alternative to
the biological family. Even in the absence of a belief
in the necessity of close cognitive and affective interaction between adult and infant for human development, it seems highly unlikely that any society would

111

have separated mother and child if the original attraction was strong and biologically based.

In the other alternative (2b) in which there would be no original biological attraction, but it would be necessary to have interaction with an adult to produce stable adults, and or, it would be so believed, it would still seem improbable that in Levy's term, a game of "musical chairs" would be a viable possibility.

Finally, let us consider the alternatives in which two of these arguments might be true, but not all three. Thus (alternative 3) it might be the case that biological mothers and their children are not attracted to each other on biological grounds, but that close cognitive and affective interaction with some adult members of the species is necessary for human development and such interaction cannot be systematically induced on a sufficient scale except with biological mothers. In such a case either psychological or social forces or both would be conceived to guarantee the necessary family structures by training biological mothers to become "good" mothers. Individual and/or social sanctions would be used to reward good mothers and to discourage biological mothers from being bad mothers. Such indeed is in fact commonly the case if the biological (or step) mother flagrantly neglects her children.

In alternative 3a it might be the case that mothers and their children are attracted to each other on biological grounds, that close interaction is, however, not necessary for human development, and that such interaction could not be developed except with biological mothers. If this were so, biological mothers would first be attracted to their own children, would naturally seek close cognitive and affective interaction, might also be reinforced in this by further so-

112

Silvan S. Tomkins

cial sanctions, but all this not be necessary for the maintenance either of a family or of a stable society. This would be one of the cases considered by Levy in which the lack of social inventiveness obscured alternative possibilities.

In alternative 3b biological mothers would be attracted to their children, close interaction with adults would be necessary for human development, but *biological* mothers would not be the only possible mothers. This is the case which Levy considered of "musical chairs" and rejected as entirely improbable. We are in agreement with his interpretation in this case, for the reason that *if* mothers were in fact biologically attracted to their children, and their children to them, and it were necessary for human development that there be close cognitive and affective interaction between adults and infants, and/or so believed, then all mothers (and their infants) would have too much to lose and too little to gain from swapping mothers and infants to make such a social institution viable.

This examination of some of the alternatives to Levy's arguments has disclosed some interesting properties of his assumptions. First, the strongest case against his arguments requires that all three assumptions be rejected—no biological attraction, no necessity for intimacy between adult and infant for human development, and no necessity for biological mothers as mothers. Second, even in the absence of a biological attraction and in the absence of a necessity for prolonged interaction for human development, it would not be likely that an alternative to the biological family could have developed in the form of a musical chairs game. It would have been particularly unlikely if it had been *believed* that prolonged interaction was necessary between adult and infant, no

113

matter what was the case in fact. Finally, if *either* close interaction is necessary or believed so, *or* there is a strong biological attraction, then it is unlikely that alternatives to the biological mother caring for her child are probable social institutions. The third argument thus appears to follow if either the first or the second are true, or believed to be true. On the other hand none of the three arguments need be true. So much for sheer possibility and the structure of these three arguments. Let us now turn to the major question. What is the truth of the matter? Do we know this? How certain can we be?

THE NATURE OF HUMAN DEVELOPMENT

The case seems to us to be very similar to that in language. Language is a biopsychosocial phenomenon in which a biological mechanism must be supported by both psychological and social forces for the language to develop. At the biological level, it is perfectly clear that complex languages of communication require a nervous system of extraordinary complexity. In those instances in which there are critical genetic defects no amount of psychosocial stimulation appears to be capable of compensating for these deficiencies at the biological level. This is not to say that deafmutes cannot be taught another form of the same language when only the voice mechanism is the locus of the deficiency. We refer rather to those human beings whose brain is so severely impaired that they seem incapable of learning language of any kind. It is equally evident that language must be learned from one who already speaks the language, that it must be practised, and for this, that it must be motivated. A hypothetical lone human being who managed somehow to grow to maturity without contact or help from any other human being would be

114

extremely unlikely to have generated a language of communication.

We will argue that human development in general is a biopsychosocial phenomenon and that it is the great virtue of Levy's arguments that he rested his case on biological, psychological, and social grounds. It is essentially a biological argument that he uses to account for the attraction between mother and child. It is a biopsychosocial argument when he argues that close cognitive and affective interaction is essential for human development, and that stable adults are required for society. It is a biopsychosocial argument when he argues that biological mothers are necessary if we are to have such interaction on a sufficiently large scale—since this is a function of both biological attraction and the past experience of having been nurtured by *their own* biological mother who had presumably provided the close cognitive and affective interaction necessary for their development. Although we stress the biopsychosocial nature of Levy's arguments, it should be noted that he tends to exaggerate the "biological" source which he explicitly labels. He also uses psychological and social arguments—as in his emphasis on the necessity of close cognitive and affective interaction for human development—but this argument is labelled neither psychological nor social. Indeed there is a hint from his third argument that this too is a derivative of the original "biological" attraction, since he thinks "such interaction with infants cannot systematically be induced except in biological mothers on a sufficient scale to produce enough stable adults and keep a society in operation." His first argument therefore is explicitly biological, and so is his third argument, but the second argument is ambiguous with respect to whether this itself is a biological, a psychological or a

The Biopsychosociality of the Family

social phenomenon. We think it is a biopsychosocial phenomenon.

Not only do we think Levy's sandwich is too much one part ambiguity surrounded by two slices of biological bread, but we think that both bread and filling are each composed of biopsychosocial components. In our restaurant the consumer would face a nine-deckered sandwich. Further, Levy's use of the word "biological" is entirely too restricted to the hormonal, drive sources of motivation.

The crux of the empirical problem concerns the nature of the mother-child relationship and the nature of human development. These are areas which are presently undergoing intensive scrutiny, and we now know much more about them than we have ever known before. But there is much we do not know, a great deal we do not know for certain, and much we think we know because of both implicit and explicit theoretical positions which are defended with sufficient piety to generate no more than equal parts of heat and illumination. This discussant is no exception to this rule. He will present evidence for and against Levy's position in the light of a theoretical model which he has presented elsewhere.[1]

THE BIOLOGY OF MOTIVATION

Let us consider first the nature of the mother-child relationship. Levy has argued "for physiological reasons biological mothers will if given the opportunity initiate interaction with their biological offspring with very high probability and the biological offspring, if given the opportunity will respond with a very high probability." Levy postulates further "that

[1] Silvan S. Tomkins, *Affect, Imagery and Consciousness*, Vol. I, Vol. II, Vol. III + IV (In Press), Springer Publishing Co., New York, N. Y., 1962-1963.

Silvan S. Tomkins

the probability of the biological mother being so motivated has to do with physiological factors such as hormonal balances at time of parturition."

It is our belief that Levy is correct in stressing the biological factors in the attraction between mother and child, but that he has misidentified the appropriate biological factors. He is operating within the framework of a psychology and biology of motivation which is no longer tenable.

In our view the primary motivational system is the affective system, and the biological drives have motivational impact only when amplified by the affective system. We are here positing, as Levy does, a biological base for the attraction between mother and child, and indeed for the attraction between any human beings, but it is not the same biological base.

Let us then examine the nature of human motivation. In a dimly lit cave one night after the day's work had been done, one of our more reflective forbears wrinkled his forehead, scratched his beard, and, in wonder and perplexity, began the study of human motivation. His answer to the fundamental question—"what do human beings really want" was the same answer that was to be given for some few thousand years up to and including Hull and Freud. That answer was, and for not a few still is, that the human animal is driven to breathe, to eat, to drink, and to sex—that the biological drives are the primary sources of motivation of all animals, not excluding man. The clarity and urgency of hunger, of thirst, of anoxia, and of lust provided the basic paradigm that captured the imagination of all theorists. Protests against this paradigm have been perennial, but none of its competitors has had its hardiness.

This is a radical error. The intensity, the urgency, the imperiousness, the "umph" of drives, is an illusion. The illusion is created by the misidentification of the drive signal with its amplifier. Its amplifier is the affective response which is ordinarily recruited to boost the gain of the drive signal.

Consider anoxic deprivation. Almost any interference with normal breathing will immediately arouse the most desperate gasping for breath. Is there any motivational claim more urgent than the demand of one who is drowning or choking to death for want of air? And yet it is not simply the imperious demand for oxygen that we observe under such circumstances. We are also observing the rapidly mounting panic ordinarily recruited whenever the air supply is suddenly jeopardized. The panic amplifies the drive signal and it is the combination of drive signal and panic which we have mistakenly identified for the drive signal. We have only to change the rate of anoxic deprivation to change the nature of the recruited affect which accompanies the anoxic drive signal. Thus, in the last war, those pilots who refused to wear their oxygen masks at 30,000 feet suffered a more gradual anoxic deprivation. They did not panic for want of oxygen. They became euphoric. It was the affect of enjoyment which the more slowly developing anoxic signal recruited. Some of these therefore met their death with a smile on their lips.

Consider next that most imperious, primary drive of sex. Surely the tumescent, erect male is driven. Surely the tumescent sexual organ is the site of both the sexual urge and sexual pleasure. So it is, but just as we misidentify panic and the anoxic signal, so here we have misidentified the tumescence of the sexual drive with the affect of excitement. Excitement is ordinarily recruited as an amplifier of the sexual drive signal. But no one has ever observed an excited penis. One is excited and breathes hard, not in the penis, but in the chest, the oesophagus, the face, and in the nose and nostrils. Both the sexual urge and the sexual pleasure of intercourse are ordinarily amplified by excitement as anoxia is amplified by panic. But the potency of the sexual drive is notoriously vulnerable to the learned recruitment of affect which inhibits sexual satisfaction. If one learns to feel ashamed or afraid of sexuality, tumescence may become impossible, and the potent primary drive becomes impotent. To be fully sexually aroused and satisfied, one must be capable of excitement as well as tumescence. The contribution of affect to complete sexual satisfaction is nowhere clearer than for those who report unimpaired sexual pleasure and even orgasm, but nonetheless complain of lack of sexual satisfaction. What can it mean when the genitals are tumescent, yield sexual pleasure from mutual stimulation which produces mutual orgasm, and yet both partners report that they are sexually unfulfilled and dissatisfied? Sexual intercourse repeated with the same partner is vulnerable to such attenuation of satisfaction whenever the decline in novelty of the interpersonal relationship is such that excitement can no longer be sustained. Those who are generally bored with each other may also be unable to become sexually excited even when they are capable of stimulating tumescence and orgasm. Excitement is no more a peculiarly sexual phenomenon, than panic is unique to anoxic deprivation.

Beach,[2] in his review of sexual behavior in mammals has shown that greater complexity has increasingly freed the more primitive sexual mechanisms from strict control by gonadal hormones. On the one

[2] Frank A. Beach, "A Review of Physiological and Psychological Studies of Sexual Behavior in Mammals," *Physiological Reviews*, Vol. 27, No. 2 (April, 1947), pp. 292-294.

The Biopsychosociality of the Family

hand he shows "there are several lines of evidence to prove that gonadal hormones exert specific and powerful effects upon sexual behavior in all mammalian forms. In seasonally-breeding species the occurence of intense and complete sexual performance coincides with periods of maximal secretory function in the testes and ovaries. In year-round breeders the male is continuously active sexually, while the female's periods of receptivity occur when mature follicles are present and the estrogen level is high. The relationship between ovarian condition and sexual behavior is clear-cut in females of lower mammalian species, but the female monkey shows some willingness to receive the male at times when the ovaries do not contain ripe follicles; and even greater emancipation from hormonal control is seen in the mating activity of the female chimpanzee, who exhibits periodicity of responsiveness but may permit copulation at any stage of the ovarian cycle. The highest degree of freedom from ovarian direction of sex desire obtains in the human female in whom non-hormonal factors exert at least equally important effects." ". . . In the course of mammalian evolution several changes in the physiological bases for sexual behavior appear to have taken place. Increase in the size and complexity of the neo-cortex has been accompanied by progressive encephalization of sensory-motor functions including many of those involved in courtship and mating. Concomitantly the sub-cerebral mechanisms which originally were capable of mediating sexual responses have come to be more and more dependent upon facilitative impulses from functionally associated circuits lying higher in the nervous system. Progressive encephalization of various sexual activities has resulted in increasing variability and modifiability, both of the types of stimuli adequate to elicit sexual activity and of the overt forms of behavior by which sexual excitement may be expressed. Finally, development of increasing dependence upon facilitation from the neopallium has in some measure freed the more primitive sexual mechanisms from strict control by gonadal hormones."

The same greater freedom from hormonal control may also be seen in maternal behavior. We must not therefore base our understanding of human maternal behavior too directly on the studies, such as those of Harlow, of maternal behavior in monkeys and chimpanzees, despite the fact that these studies are of *some* relevance for understanding human maternal behavior.

Beach has not stressed as much as we have the central role of affect in sexual behavior. We are, however, entirely in agreement with the position he has stated. In addition, however, we would urge that the affect of excitement, itself activated by ideation and phantasy, mediates the sexual drive by amplifying, modulating, or attenuating it. Levy has exaggerated the drive and hormonal influence in maternal behavior, and overlooked the critical *biological* role of the affects and the higher mental processes.[3]

The biological substrate of motivation has been further illuminated in recent years by the discovery of subcortical structures, such as the reticular formation, which are largely responsible for the main-

[3] Conversations with Levy disclosed that his equation of biological with drive and hormonal factors was based on lack of information of alternative biological mechanisms rather than upon a wish to restrict alternatives. It is safe to assume that Levy's assumptions are fairly general among social scientists including many psychologists.

tenance of the state of wakefulness, alertness, and consciousness. Thus anaesthesia is possible despite the fact that pain messages continue to be transmitted to the brain, because the anaesthetic inhibits the reticular formation so that it fails to provide the additional amplification which would make the individual conscious of pain.

The relationship we have postulated between the drive system and the affect system must therefore also be postulated between both of these and non-specific amplifying systems, such as the reticular formation. This and other amplifier circuits serve both motivational and nonmotivational systems. The words commonly used in this connection, activation and arousal, have tended to confound the distinction between amplification from affects and the non-specific amplification of any neural message, be it a sensory, motor, drive, or affect message. Amplification is the preferable, more generic term, since it describes equally well the increase or decrease in gain for any and every kind of message or structure. The terms activation and arousal should be abandoned because of their affective connotations.

It is now clear from the work of Sprague, Chambers, and Stellar [4] that it is possible by appropriate anatomical lesion to produce a cat who is active by virtue of intact amplifier structures but who shows little affect and conversely, to produce a cat who is inactive, and drowsy, but who responds readily with affect to mild stimulation. "Thus it appears that after interruption of much of the classical, lemniscal paths at the rostral midbrain, the cat shows . . . little attention and affect despite the fact that the animal is

[4] J. M. Sprague, W. W. Chambers, and E. Stellar, "Attentive, Affective, and Adaptive Behavior in the Cat," *Science,* Vol. 133, No. 3447 (January, 1961), pp. 165-173.

wakeful and active and has good motor capacity.
. . . These cats are characterized by a *lack of affect*, showing little or no defensive and aggressive reaction to noxious and aversive situations and no response to pleasurable stimulation or solicitation of
affection by petting. The animals are mute, lack
facial expression, and show minimal autonomic responses. . . . Without a patterned afferent input to
the forebrain via the lemnisci, the remaining portions of the central nervous system, which include a
virtually intact reticular formation, seem incapable
of elaborating a large part of the animal's repertoire
of adaptive behavior. . . . In contrast to this picture, a large reticular lesion sparing the lemnisci
results in an animal whose general behavior is much
like that of a normal cat except for chronic hypo-
kinesia or drowsiness and for strong and easily
aroused affect to mild stimulation."

Both drives and affects require non-specific amplification, but the drives have insufficient strength
as motives without concurrent amplification by both
the affects and the nonspecific amplifiers. Their critical role is to provide information—vital information,
of place, and of response—where and when to do
what when the body does not know how to otherwise
help itself. When the drive signal is activated we
learn first when we must start and stop consummatory activity. We become hungry long before our
tissues are in an emergency state of deficit and we
stop eating, due to satiety, long before the tissue deficit has been remedied.

But there is also information of place and of response—where to do what. When the drive is activated it tells us a very specific story—that the
"problem" is in the mouth in the case of hunger, far-
ther back in the throat in thirst, in the finger or

wherever we have hurt ourselves in the case of pain, in the nose and throat and chest if it is an oxygen drive, in the urethra if it is the urination drive, at the anal sphincter if it is the defecation drive. This information has been built into the site of consummation so the probability of finding the correct consummatory response is very high. That this information is as vital as the message *when* to eat can be easily exposed.

Let us suppose that the hunger drive were rewired to be localized in the urethra, and the sex drive localized in the palm of the hand. For sexual satisfaction the individual would first open and close his hand and then reach for a wide variety of "objects" as possible satisfiers, cupping and rubbing his hand until orgasm. When he became hungry he might first release the urethra and urinate to relieve his hunger. If this did not relieve it, he might use his hands to find objects which might be put inside the urethra, depending on just how we had rewired the apparatus. Such an organism would be neither viable nor reproducible. Such specificity of time and place of the drive system, critical though it is for viability is, nevertheless, a limitation on its general significance for the human being.

It is the affects, rather than the drives, which are the primary human motives. First because the drives require amplification from the affects, whereas the affects are sufficient motivators in the absence of drives. One must be excited to be sexually aroused, but one need not be sexually aroused to be excited. It is quite sufficient to motivate any man, to arouse either excitement or joy or terror or anger or shame or contempt or distress or surprise.

Second, in contrast to the specificity of the space-time information of the drive system, the affect system has those more general properties which permit it to assume a central position in the motivation of man. Thus, the affect system has generality of time rather than the rhythmic specificity of the drive system. Because the drive system is essentially a transport system, taking material in and out of the body, it must impose its specific temporal rhythms, strictly. One cannot breathe on Tuesday, Thursday and Saturday, but one *could* be happy on Tuesday, Thursday, and Saturday and sad on Monday, Wednesday, and Friday.

In contrast to the necessary constraints of a system which enjoys few degrees of freedom in transporting material in and out of the body, there is nothing inherent in the structure of the affect mechanism which limits its activation with respect to time. One can be anxious for just a moment or for half an hour, or for a day, or for a month, or for a year, or a decade, or a lifetime, or *never*, or only occasionally now though much more frequently some time ago, or conversely.

There are also structures in the body which are midway between the drive and affect mechanisms. Thus the pain receptors on the back of my hand are as site specific as any drive. *If* I were to place a cigarette on the skin of my hand, I would experience pain. But the pain mechanism is similar to the affect mechanism in its time generality. There is nothing in the nature of the pain receptors which requires that it be stimulated rhythmically, or that it ever be stimulated, and nothing which would prevent them from being stimulated whenever I happened to have an accident.

The affect sysem also permits generality or freedom of object. Although one may satisfy hunger by Chinese, American, or Italian food, it must be some

The Biopsychosociality of the Family

variety of edible object. Not so with any affect. There is literally no kind of object which has not been linked to one or another of the affects. In masochism man has even learned to love pain and death. In puritanism he has learned to hate pleasure and life. He can invest any and every aspect of existence with the magic of excitement and joy or with the dread of fear or shame or distress.

Affects also are capable of much greater generality of intensity than drives. If I do not eat I become hungrier and hungrier. As I eat I become less hungry. But I may wake mildly irritable in the morning and remain so for the rest of the day. Or, one day I may not be at all angry until quite suddenly something makes me explode in a rage. I may start the day moderately angry and quickly become interested in some other matter and so dissipate my anger.

Not only are both intensity and duration of affect capable of greater modulation than is possible for drives, but so is their density. By *affect density* we mean the product of intensity times duration. Most of the drives operate within relatively narrow density tolerances. The consequence of too much variation of density of intake of air is loss of consciousness and possible death. Compared with drives, affects may be either much more casual and low in density or much more monopolistic and high in density. By virtue of the flexibility of this system man is enabled to oscillate between affect finickiness, fickleness of purpose, and obsessive possession by the object of his affective investments.

Not only may affects be widely invested and variously invested, but they may also be invested in other affects, combine with other affects, intensify or modulate them, and suppress or reduce them. Neither

126

Silvan S. Tomkins

hunger nor thirst can be used to reduce the need for air, nor conversely, as, for example, a child may be shamed into crying, or may be shamed into stopping crying.

The basic power of the affect system is a consequence of its freedom to combine with a variety of other components in what we have called a *central assembly*. This is an executive mechanism upon which messages converge from all sources, competing from moment to moment for inclusion in this governing central assembly. The affect system can be both evoked by central and peripheral messages from any source, and in turn control the disposition of such messages and their sources.

The possibility of man as the variously socialized and acculturated entity we know him to be, depends we think on the flexibility of the primary biological motivational mechanisms—the affect system. This biological substrate exerts some constraints on human development, but it also makes the varieties of human development in different societies possible. It is the strength of Levy's argument to have emphasized the close interdependence of biological, psychological, and social forces. He is mistaken however in supposing that hormonal based drives irresistibly draw the mother to her child in the tropistic fashion of the moth drawn to the flame, or in the manner even of a monkey drawn to her infant. There is indeed a strong tie between mother and infant which has biological roots, but before we can fully understand its nature we will have to examine further the nature of the affect system.

If the affects are our primary motives, what are they and where are they? Affects are sets of muscle and glandular responses located in the face and also widely distributed through the body, which generate

The Biopsychosociality of the Family

sensory feedback which is either inherently "acceptable" or "unacceptable." These organized sets of responses are triggered at subcortical centers where specific "programs" for each distinct affect are stored. These programs are innately endowed and have been genetically inherited. They are capable, when activated, of simultaneously capturing such widely distributed organs as the face, the heart, and the endocrines and imposing on them a specific pattern of correlated responses. One does not learn to be afraid, or to cry, or to startle, any more than one learns to feel pain or to gasp for air. The organism is so constructed that the awareness of joy is more acceptable than the awareness of fear. These are the basic wants and don't wants of the human being. They are "ends-in-themselves," positive and negative. These are primarily aesthetic experiences. The human being passively enjoys or suffers these experiences before he is capable of either approach or escape or maximizing or minimizing them through instrumental behavior. What to "do" about these experiences cannot be altogether clear to the neonate who is relatively incompetent to do very much about anything. Although these constitute the basic wants and don't wants of the human being, it is only gradually that they can become the targets for the feedback control system. It is a long step from the consummatory pleasure of eating and the affect of joy at the sight of the mother's face to the "wish" for these, and a still longer step to the instrumental behaviors necessary to satisfy any wish. Nonetheless there is a high probability that the human being will ultimately utilize his feedback mechanisms to maximize his positive affects, such as excitement and joy, and to minimize his negative affects such as distress, fear, and shame.

Silvan S. Tomkins

The human being's ability to maintain and reproduce himself is guaranteed not only by a responsiveness to drive signals but by a responsiveness to whatever circumstances activate positive and negative affect. Some of the triggers to interest, joy, distress, startle, disgust, aggression, fear, and shame are unlearned. At the same time the affect system is also capable of being instigated by learned stimuli. In this way the human being is born biased toward and away from a limited set of circumstances and is also capable of learning to acquire new objects of interest and disinterest. By means of a variety of innate activators of these wanted or unwanted responses and their feedback reports, the human being is urged to explore and attempt to control the circumstances which seem to evoke his positive and negative affective responses. We say "seem" because the individual may or may not correctly identify these activators. Thus one usually correctly identifies the source of panic when there is insufficient air being inspired, but may fail to identify the same source when this deprivation is experienced at a slower rate and the individual dies in a state of euphoria.

The price that is paid for this flexibility is ambiguity and error. The individual may or may not correctly identify the "cause" of his fear or joy and may or may not learn to reduce his fear or maintain or recapture his joy. In this respect the affect system is not as simple a signal system as the drive system. If the feedback of the affective response is motivating, then whatever instigates, maintains, and reduces the affect can also become equally motivating. To the extent that there are invariant relationships between any stimulus and any affect, that stimulating state of affairs can become the sign of that affect. The face which frightens the child can become

The Biopsychosociality of the Family

the fear-causing face and eventually the to-be-avoided face. So long as the instigator of the affect is correctly identified, any inborn, invariant relationship between instigator and affect guarantees that the former becomes motivating.

Let us now examine some of the recent empirical evidence for the motivational power of the affect system.

RECENT FINDINGS ON THE AFFECT SYSTEM

One of the most revolutionary findings in the recent past was the discovery of the joy and aversive centers of the brain. These are areas the electrical stimulation of which the animal appears to want or reject, and for which he will exert himself strenuously and continuously. Psychologists working with rats have been very tentative in interpreting the nature of these rewards and punishments except to state, as Olds [5] did, that they necessitate a revision in the drive theory of motivation and learning.

It would appear to us that these are structures which contain innate, quite specific affect programs for the control of facial muscles and autonomic organs. Partly because much of this experimental work involves rats and partly because of a shyness about identifying behavioral responses with the conscious correlates of their feedback, until now this evidence has not been interpreted in terms of an affect theory of motivation.

Such evidence as we have from analogous stimulation of humans is highly suggestive that stimula-

[5] James Olds, "Physiological mechanisms of reward," *Nebraska Symposium on Motivation, 1955,* edited by Marshall R. Jones (Lincoln, Neb. Univ. Nebraska Press, 1955), pp. 73-138.

Silvan S. Tomkins

tion of these areas produces the responses the feedback of which are consciously experienced as affects.

Heath[6] has stated that, in brain stimulation of humans under local anaesthetic, there were reports of experienced feelings correlated with specific site stimulation and with widespread autonomic responses.

With stimulation to the more rostral midline structures, i.e., the septal region, patients appear alerted, speak more rapidly and state that they feel quite comfortable.

Stimuli delivered more caudally so as to involve the rostral hypothalamus result in complaints of discomfort and there is marked stimulation of the peripheral autonomics. Patients complain of discomfort, fullness in the head, pounding heart and so on.

Stimulation through either the septal region or rostral hypothalamus has usually resulted in the physiological effect of a marked drop of circulating eosinophils and lymphocytes, usually associated with a marked increase in the total white cell count and no change in the total red cell count.

With stimulation of the caudal diencephalon and the region of the tegmentum of the mesencephalon, the patients have developed diffuse tension and rage and complained of diplopia (double vision) due to stimulation spread to the third nuclei.

The same parameters of stimulation, which produce a drop in eosinophils when applied in the septal region and rostral hypothalamus, when applied through the caudate region were usually not associated with eosinopenia or lymphopenia (i.e.,

[6] R. G. Heath, "Correlations between levels of psychological awareness and physiological activity in the central nervous system," *Psychosomat. Med.*, Vol. 17 (1955), pp. 383-395.

decrease); often a mild eosinophilia and lymphophilia (i.e., increase) resulted.

Changes in the number of circulating eosinophils and lymphocytes following stimulation to the more caudal midline structures, i.e., the mesencephalic tegmentum, were considerably less marked than those which appeared with the septal and rostral hypothalamic stimulation.

Stimulation of the amygdaloid nucleus resulted in an intense emotional reaction which varied from one stimulation to the next in the same patient although parameters of stimulation were consistent. Sometimes it produced a reaction of rage and at other times a reaction of fear. The patient's description was "I don't know what came over me. I felt like an animal."

Stimulation of the hippocampus has produced anxiety and in one patient a *déjà vu* phenomenon. Although stimulation of the amygdaloid and hippocampus was accompanied by subjective emotion, it produced little alteration in the chemical measurements.

Although there is reference to being comfortable and alert, indicating that perhaps the affect of interest was stimulated, it would appear that these explorations missed the site of the smile response and the joy center.

There is an unanswered question in the mapping of the rat's brain: whether excitement and joy can be differentiated and whether in such a lower form there are two distinct positive affects. Since the smiling response in man is distinct from the laughing response, whereas they are not so distinct in some of the less advanced primates, it is altogether reasonable to suppose that the joy center in the rat constitutes one general positive affect rather than, as

Silvan S. Tomkins

in man, a more specific positive affect differentiated from excitement.

That these centers are related to autonomic response is reported by Hess,[7] who has shown that in the cat electrical stimulation in a dorsoposterior system in the hypothalamus produces sympathetic responses and that electrical stimulation in a ventro-anterior system in the hypothalamus produces parasympathetic responses.

Olds, Travis and Schwing[8] present data which suggest that the stimulation of the Hess areas of parasympathetic effects produce reward of behavior and that stimulation of the Hess areas of sympathetic effects may produce punishment of behavior.

Let us examine now some of the major findings on self-stimulation of the brain in rats. In these studies the electrical stimulation of the rat's brain through implanted electrodes was made to be contingent upon the actions of the rat. Thus, insofar as the electrical stimulation was either pleasant or unpleasant, it served as a reward or punishment for the rat's actions. According to Olds, healthy well-fed rats running for a brain shock reward endured far more painful shock to the feet than did the 24-hour-hungry rats running for food. The drive for self-stimulation appeared to be (in some cases) at least twice as strong as a 24-hour hunger drive. Animals with electrodes on the telencephalon appeared to show some genuine satiation. No similar satiation appeared in animals with electrodes in the hypothalamus.

When animals were run for periods of an hour a

[7] W. R. Hess, *The Functional Organization of the Diencephalon* (New York: Grune & Stratton, 1958).

[8] J. Olds, R. D. Travis, and R. C. Schwing, "Topographic organization of hypothalamic self-stimulation functions," *J. Comp. Physiol. Psychol.*, Vol. 53 (1960), pp. 23-32.

day they usually maintained the same rate of self-stimulation throughout the hour and for as many days or months as they were tested.

If animals with electrodes implanted in the hypothalamus were run for 24 hours or 48 hours consecutively, they continued to respond as long as physiological endurance permitted.

Rats with electrodes implanted in the telencephalon, on the other hand, seemed to slow down considerably when they were shifted from a one to a twenty-four hour self-stimulation schedule.

The extensive reward system appears to break down into subsystems subservient to the different basic drives; there appears to be a food-reward system, a sex-reward system, and so on.

If electrode stimulation at some points fires cells that mediate food reward, the animal's appetite for self-stimulation at this point may go up and down with hunger as its appetite for food does.

When tests were made at a constant current of 65 microamperes with a set of electrodes placed in the midline of the brain, in the ventromedial hypothalamus and in the septal area, hunger seemed to have an important positive effect, increasing self-stimulation rates.

When, however, animals were tested at a series of current levels, a somewhat different picture of the hunger system appeared. Animals were run alternately—one day hungry and the next day full—to see whether this would change the rate of self-stimulation during the various intervals. Many animals responded faster when hungry and slower when sated, but this difference appeared only at a limited range of electric shock levels.

The rewarding stimulus often appears to produce a temporary increment in some consummatory behavior. Stimulation in the ventral posterior hypo-thalamus at points about 1.5 millimeters lateral to the midline caused an increase in eating.

After these tests were completed the same animals were subjected to self-stimulation tests with the same levels of current. The lateral electrode placements, in areas where stimulation seemed to increase hunger drive, were the ones that usually produced extremely high rates of self-stimulation. Olds comments on the anachronism for drive reduction theory in the fact that electrical stimulation at one site will both increase eating behavior and the self-stimulation rate in the absence of food. If we assume that in the rat, the affect for eating is as specifically activated as excitement is by sexual stimulation in the case of man, then the paradox disappears.

Olds has also found that the area which produces avoidance behavior is small compared with that which produces approach behavior. The actual rate of bar pressing for brain stimulation was as high as 7,000 per hour. There is an orderly arrangement of the rewarding effect in the rhinencephalon and related structures such that the response rates decline as stimulation is moved forward toward the cortex.

He found also that if the rate of responding for brain stimulation increased as the strength of the brain shock is increased, he could estimate the size of the sphere surrounding a point of stimulation in which electric stimulation is rewarding. When the size of this sphere is large, the rate of self-stimulation at high current levels is very high. When it is a small area the rate, even at high current levels, is low.

There are also studies which show that electrical stimulation in some areas has both rewarding and punishing effects, depending on the duration and intensity of stimulation. This may account for the finding which W. W. Roberts[9] reported that stimulation in the posterior hypothalamus of a cat will persuade the animal to enter one maze alley if this response is followed by the switching on of the current, and to enter another alley about ten seconds later to have the current switched off.

When the stimulating voltage was relatively weak, it appeared to be primarily rewarding. When the voltage was increased it became punishing, the animal seeking to escape stimulation.

Olds[10] has also, more recently, answered the question of the relationship between reward and punishment on the one hand, and arousal or non-specific amplification on the other. He found that these functions are mediated by distinct sites and structures. This is what one would expect in view of the independent role of affective amplification and the more general non-specific amplification which forms the basis for the difference between more and less wakefulness, more and less consciousness.

Such brain stimulation can be used to establish secondary reinforcement. Stein[11] showed that a neutral stimulus, a tone, would be worked for by bar pressing, following pairing of the tone with the brain shock.

Let us return now to the question of the relationship between brain stimulation and affect.

[9] W. W. Roberts, "Both rewarding and punishing effects from stimulation of posterior hypothalamus with same electrode at same intensity," *J. Comp. Physiol. Psychol.*, Vol. 51 (1958), pp. 400-407.

[10] J. Olds, "Self-stimulation of the brain," *Science*, Vol. 127 (1958), pp. 315-324.

[11] Larry Stein, "Secondary reinforcement established with subcortical stimulation," *Science,* Vol. 127 (1958), pp. 466-467.

Silvan S. Tomkins

As Brady and Conrad [12] recently observed, surprisingly little attention has been given to the affective changes related to positively rewarding brain stimulation. Its relation to stimulus intensity, schedules of reinforcement, food and water deprivation, hormones, drugs and satiation effects have been studied and reported. We can only suppose that the magical use of the word reinforcement is in part responsible for the failure of one of the most important discoveries of this century to be fully exploited theoretically.

This failure is due first to the assimilation of this discovery to drive theory or to conditioning theory so that it becomes still another drive, or still another technique of the experimental control of behavior. Its first startle value has become habituated and it appears now to constitute no serious threat either to drive theory or to a variety of conditioning theories.

In the second place, its failure to be exploited derives from its positive nature. Although we are accustomed to food as a reinforcer, it is the reduction of the negative hunger drive which is held to be the true reinforcer, rather than the pleasure of eating. There is an enduring strain of Puritanism in learning theory which prompts avoidance and devaluation of positive reinforcement. The notion that positive stimulation per se can motivate has been for American psychology a bitter pill which has not yet been swallowed with pleasure. Skinnerian emphasis on positive reinforcement entirely produced and controlled by the experimenter is the boldest reach achieved so far. But here we deal with an empty or-

[12] J. V. Brady, "A comparative approach to the experimental analysis of emotional behavior," in *Experimental Psychopathology,* edited by P. Hoch and J. Zubin (New York: Grune & Stratton, 1957).

ganism and a full experimenter who is determined to avoid awareness of these internal responses which constitute the foundation of positive reinforcement.

Brady and Conrad have examined the effects of limbic system self-stimulation on what they call "conditioned emotional behavior."

They trained rats, cats, and monkeys in lever pressing for both brain shock reinforcement and water and food. After this had been established they employed the following emotional conditioning procedure: they sounded a clicking noise for a fixed interval for 3 or 5 minutes, which was terminated contiguously with a brief, painful electric shock to the animal's feet. Chronic electrodes had been implanted in the limbic system of all animals.

The three rats who had been trained in lever pressing for a water reward and then emotionally conditioned to the clicker-shock combination stopped pressing the lever during the clicker sound. When they were switched to brain shock reward on the same variable interval reinforcement schedule, the lever pressing rate returned to a stable level comparable to that during the original water reward period before the emotional conditioning to the clicker-shock combination.

The first presentation of the clicker (without shock) during a brain shock reinforcement session, within one week after the last emotional conditioning trial, failed to suppress the lever pressing rate in any of the three rats. This virtually complete attenuation of the conditioned fear response continued for all three rats throughout eight succeeding pairings of clicker and shock during electrical self-stimulation. One of these rats was tested in this fashion for thirty-two experimental sessions and still showed no conditioned fear responses. The other two rats were not tested beyond eight trials. All three rats were then continued on a testing schedule which alternated water and brain stimulation daily with daily fear conditioning trials. When the animals worked for water reward, the clicker lowered the rate of lever pressing. When the animals worked for brain stimulation all three rats worked through the clicker and showed no fear response.

Finally, after fourteen days on this alternate-day testing procedure one rat was tested during a single 2-hour experimental session with alternating 30-minute periods of lever pressing for a water reward and lever pressing for a brain stimulation reward. During each of these 30-minute cycles there was also a clicker-shock trial. Again the clicker depressed the lever pressing rate while it had no effect on the pressing for brain stimulation.

The remaining three other rats were initially trained in lever pressing for the reward of electrical stimulation to the brain. All animals developed relatively stable response rates on a variable-interval reinforcement schedule. In marked contrast to the rats who had been initially trained and fear-conditioned on the water reinforcement schedule, none of these animals developed the fear response during the initial series of eight acquisition trials, despite repeated clicker-pain shock stimulation. One rat in this group continued to receive pairings of clicker-pain shock to the feet during daily lever-pressing sessions for brain stimulation. After twenty-three additional trials with this animal there was partial suppression of the lever-pressing rate.

Following the eighth emotional conditioning trial, the other two rats were switched to water rewarded lever pressing and given eight additional fear conditioning trials. Under these conditions they did develop the conditioned suppression pattern in response to the clicker during the eight succeeding water-reinforcement lever-pressing trials.

Two cats acquired the conditioned fear response superimposed on milk reinforcements schedule. They were then placed on a schedule of brain stimulation on one day and milk reward on alternate days. When the conditioned fear stimulus was introduced during the sixth brain stimulation session both cats completely stopped pressing the lever. Premature breaking of the electrode leads prevented further systematic testing of these animals, but what testing was possible was consistent with these results.

With respect to the difference of results obtained with their rats and those obtained with their two cats, Brady and Conrad suggest that difference of electrode placement may be responsible. They leave open the possibility of such alternative explanation as species differences. They found in their monkeys that differential electrode placement produced marked differential effects of intra-cranial self-stimulation on the conditioned fear response.

With four monkeys, development of a stable suppression pattern in response to presentation of the conditioned fear stimulus required many more pairings of clicker and shock than in either the cats or the rats. After training for food reward, and then fear conditioning, followed by brain stimulation reward trials, all four monkeys showed attenuation of the fear response when the clicker was presented during brain stimulation reward. With one monkey the alternating day experiment performed with the rats was repeated with essentially the same results as described.

In another experiment, Brady reports a conditioning procedure in which the positively rewarding brain stimulation was used as the unconditioned stimulus in place of the usual painful shock to the feet. This procedure involved presentation of the conditioned clicker stimulus for repeated five-minute intervals while the animal lever-pressed for a variable interval water reward. Each stimulus presentation was terminated contiguously with a single intracranial electric shock delivered via a rewarding electrode placement in the septal region. The rat had no previous history of lever pressing for brain shock, and direct correlation between a lever response and the intracranial electrical stimulus was prevented by requiring an interval of at least two seconds following a response before the brain shock could be delivered and the clicker terminated. The consequence of this was that the slope of the lever-pressing curve showed a sharp increase during the five-minute clicker intervals as compared with the base line rates developed during the twenty minute interclicker intervals. In other words the effect of a signal of impending rewarding brain stimulation in effect summated with the anticipated water reward to increase the instrumental responses.

Thus we see that in rats and monkeys the rewarding stimulation within the limbic system successfully interferes with a conditioned fear response, and does so more successfully than drive reward (water or food). Further, it interferes not only with competing fear responses to stimuli which have already been conditioned but also *prevents* the *acquisition* of fear responses to painful electrical stimulation to the feet. This is quite similar to the effect of the clinging of the infant monkey to its surrogate cloth mother that Harlow reported. The difference

The Biopsychosociality of the Family

here is that by brain stimulation the joy center is stimulated directly rather than as a consequence of clinging to a soft cloth mother.

On the other hand, there was no effect of brain stimulation on conditioned fear responses which outlasted the actual period of self-stimulation of the brain. Finally, we have seen that the rewarding brain stimulation will *increase* the instrumental response to a drive reward summating with it. Thus, the effects of rewarding brain stimulation seems to be the instigation of an intense positive affect, which interferes with the competing affect of fear and amplifies a simultaneous drive reward.

Very recently, Malmo[13] has reported a critical finding on the effect of septal self-stimulation in rats on the heart rate. Apart from the behavioral evidence we have already examined, this is the first evidence after that presented by Hess which gives us a strong indication of what kind of positive affect is activated in rats by electrical stimulation of the septal area. Malmo found that the heart rate, recorded continuously from rats trained to press a bar for intracranial stimulation of their septal areas, fell consistently after brain stimulation. He interprets these results as evidence that the rewarding effect may be produced by a parasympathetic, quieting reaction of the autonomic nervous system to septal stimulation. This is consistent with the findings of Brady and Nauta[14] that the surgical removal of the septal area produces a hyperactive animal.

[13] R. B. Malmo, "Slowing of heart rate after septal self-stimulation in rats," *Science*, Vol. 133 (1961), pp. 1,128-1,130.

[14] J. Brady and J. H. Nauta, "Sub-cortical mechanisms in emotional behavior: affective changes following septal forebrain lesions in the albino rat," *J. Comp. Physiol. Psychol.*, Vol. 46 (1953), pp. 339-346.

Silvan S. Tomkins

In terms of our theory of the activation of excitement by an increase in stimulation, and the activation of enjoyment by a decrease in stimulation, these findings suggest that the septal area is an *enjoyment* center rather than an excitement center, inasmuch as it is associated with slowing of the heart rate rather than its increase. Second, it suggests that in the rat at least, the conditions which activate the enjoyment response may be similar to the further consequences of the enjoyment response, so that reduction of stimulation produces an affective response which itself produces further reduction of the response-produced feedback. Theoretically such a circular relationship would accelerate the relaxation of the animal in deepening enjoyment if the reduction of heart rate is again a further stimulus for the activation of the enjoyment center which would then further slow the heart rate. Theoretically it should be possible to put a baby or an adult to sleep in this way, and successive soothing which produces relaxed enjoyment does in fact seem to operate by such a circular mechanism.

If our primary motives are based upon inherited programs located in subcortical centers, we should expect that not all animals would have evolved the same affects, or at the very least not with identical strengths. This consideration is critical in the evaluation of Levy's argument concerning the biological attraction between mother and infant and with respect to the more general problem posed—namely the biological base of social responsiveness in general. Let us therefore review the evidence for the evolution of the affects, with special attention to the inheritance of social responsiveness.

The Biopsychosociality of the Family

Modern evolutionary theory portrays man as an adapted organism, fearfully and wonderfully made, but also imperfectly adapted because he is a patchwork thrown together, bit by bit, without a plan, and remodeled opportunistically as occasions permitted. The conjoint operation of blind mutation, genetic recombination, and natural selection contrived that magnificent makeshift, the human being.

There is a consensus according to Simpson that it is the population of genes rather than the genes of any individual which is governed by natural selection. Since a population maintains itself by diversity of genes, every variant (particular combination of genes) need not maintain itself any more than a single individual ceases to exist because he is continually replacing aging tissue, e.g., his skin. Secondly, in some contrast to Darwin's views, natural selection by reproduction is held to be the only nonrandom selective factor. The problem of adaptation then has shifted somewhat from the problem how does an individual "survive" to how does a population of genes maintain itself through correlations between reproductive success and adaptation. From this position, in addition to a strong sex drive, such characteristics as sensitivity to novel stimuli, sensitivity to social stimuli, aggressiveness, timidity, and other affects become no less important foci for natural selection than the development of a homeostatic autonomic system and an adapted drive system. The individual must not only survive—he must reproduce himself in such quantity that his kind continues to reproduce itself. This continuity is vulnerable to many threats, ranging from attacks by other animals

Silvan S. Tomkins

on adults as well as on the very young, famine, floods, diseases, sterility, and so on.

It is not surprising that increasing curiosity and intelligence and social responsiveness and cooperativeness should have been selected in many species by virtue of the correlation between the adaptive advantages of these characteristics and reproductive success. H. J. Muller[15] has suggested that natural selection favors social cooperation in those situations in which an individual in helping others assists in the survival of its own genes, or the same or similar genes in the other individuals. One such case is the nurturing and protecting of the young. On the other hand, where a way of life puts a premium on early dispersal of the young, maternal care and the social responsiveness of the infant to this care are minimal and are replaced by individualism and competition. Other circumstances which favor selection for social responsiveness are those in which organisms are relatively defenseless individually but are capable of dealing with predators collectively.

Despite our ignorance of the specific gene or sets of genes involved in such general characteristics as responsiveness to novel stimuli, or to specifically social stimuli, it has been possible for some time to breed animals for these and other even more specific affective and behavioral characteristics. Tryon[16] was able to breed rats who were unusual in their ability to run mazes successfully. Scott[17] noted that in selec-

[15] H. J. Muller, "Human values in relation to evolution," *Science*, Vol. 127 (1958), pp. 625-629.

[16] R. C. Tryon, "Individual differences," in F. A. Moss (ed.), *Comparative Psychology* (New York: Prentice-Hall, 1942), pp. 330-365.

[17] John Paul Scott, *Animal Behavior* (Chicago: Univ. of Chicago Press, 1958).

tion of dogs for presence or absence of aggressiveness there was an additional effect upon the social differentiation of behavior. Thus, terriers have been selected to attack game and each other, whereas hounds were selected to run in packs, to avoid fights, and to find game. Terriers turn out to have a tight dominance hierarchy among themselves whereas beagles and cocker spaniels do not display a strict dominance hierarchy among themselves. In the aggressive strains there is a greater differentiation between dominant and subordinate individuals.

Scott has noted another consequence of selection for finding game. He compared the tendency of various breeds of dogs to fixate their behavior and adopt stereotyped simple habits of taking alternate right or left turns in a maze. The maze was made of wire and the animal could solve it by visual inspection. The actual pattern of the maze called for one right, two left, and three right turns. Most of the dogs simplified it to alternate right and left turns, which got them into blind alleys. Beagles of all the breeds studied were least likely to form such stereotyped habits in this situation. Scott attributed this to the fact that beagles have been selected for their ability to find rabbits—which necessarily involves continuing alertness and responsiveness to the ever changing spatial position of the pursued rabbit.

Other animals are frequently more specialized than man in either their social or individualistic orientation. The dog in particular has been bred in some cases for sensitivity to the inanimate environment and in other cases for responsiveness to man as well as for aggressiveness and many other kinds of affective specialization. An experiment by Freed-

Silvan S. Tomkins

man[18] is most illuminating of the importance of the relative strength of the joy affect versus the excitement affect in the strength of affectional ties that are possible between man and dog.

Freedman has shown that there are significant interactions between the effect of environmental influences and constitutional differences in the rearing of different breeds of dogs. He reared eight litters of four pups each. There were two litters of Shetland sheep dogs, basenjis, wire-haired terriers, and beagles.

Within each breed, after weaning at three weeks of age, one member of a pair of dogs—matched as closely as possible on relevant variables—was disciplined and the other was indulged during two daily 15-minute periods from their third to their eighth week of age. Indulgence consisted of encouraging a pup in any activity it initiated such as play, aggression, or climbing on the supine handler. The disciplined pups were first restrained in the experimenter's lap and were later taught to sit, to stay, and to come upon command.

At eight weeks of age each pup was subjected to the following procedure: each time a pup ate meat from a bowl placed in the center of a room, he was punished with a swat on the rump and a shout of "No!" After three minutes the experimenter left the room, and observing through a one-way screen, recorded the time that elapsed before the pup ate again.

He found that the basenjis ate soon after the experimenter left, and the indulged and the disciplined

18 D. G. Freedman, "Constitutional and environmental interactions in rearing of four breeds of dogs," *Science*, Vol. 127 (1958), pp. 585-586.

147

dogs did not differ in this respect. The method of rearing had had no differential effect. The Shetland sheep dogs tended to refuse the food over the entire eight days of testing. But here also there was no differential effect of rearing. The disciplined and the indulged Shetland dogs refused the food alike. With the beagles and wire-haired terriers, on the other hand, differences in rearing were critical. In the case of both breeds, the indulged pups took longer to return to the food than did the disciplined pups.

The different innate characteristics of these breeds, Freedman suggests, can account for these differences. Thus the basenjis were interested in all phases of the environment, and often ignored the experimenter in favor of inanimate objects. When they were frightened by the experimenter neither the affect of fear nor the affect of joy in response to the experimenter offered any serious long-term competition to the dominant affect of interest in the inanimate environment. Indulgence presumably permitted this breed to follow its natural inclination, but discipline neither made the animal fearful nor more socially responsive to the experimenter. When free of the presence of the experimenter the animal was able to throw off the effects of past restraint and follow the dictates of its dominant mode of orientation—to explore the environment and, in particular, to satisfy its hunger.

Shetland sheep dogs generally had become fearful of physical contact with the experimenter and tended to maintain distance from him. Inasmuch as the affect of fear, especially in respect to man, proved dominant over interest in the inanimate environment and over joy in interaction with the experimenter, the method of rearing again had no differential effect. Just as the basenjis ate because their general interest minimized the punishment from the experimenter, so with the Shetland sheep dog the fear of punishment from the experimenter was strong enough to override differences which might have been produced by indulgence or discipline and thus neither group would eat even though the experimenter was not present.

The beagles and the wire-haired terriers were strongly and positively oriented to the experimenter and sought contact with him continuously. In the case of both of these breeds past indulgence resulted in inhibition of eating under the experimental conditions and past discipline did not. We would account for this difference in the following way. For both indulged and disciplined beagles and wire-haired terriers, the positive affect responsible for social responsiveness toward the experimenter is dominant. Whatever fear of man is latent in these animals is attenuated in the case of the disciplined pups by having been accustomed gradually to interference with their wishes by discipline. Since their social affect was dominant, these dogs continued to seek interaction with the experimenter despite restraint by him. When the experimenter left, being hungry and being unafraid, they ate. We may presume that their discipline did not extend to behavior which was outside the range of behavior enforced by the experimenter's presence.

In the case of the indulged pups we would suggest that the dominant social affect was much reinforced and the latent fear of man masked by the predominant positive treatment by the experimenter. Upon being first punished by their friend the latent fear of man was aroused but not habituated since the experimenter each time left the dog alone. This fear, like the perpetual timidity of the Shetland dogs, was sufficient to inhibit their eating.

There is evidence from later experiments with these same dogs which suggests that not only did this small series of punishments have a differential temporary frightening effect on the indulged beagles and wire-haired terriers but that there was also a massive long-term, but delayed, effect. This effect did not appear in both socially responsive breeds, but only in one. The indulged beagles, in contrast to the disciplined beagles and all other breeds regardless of treatment, developed shyness of man and the experimenter.

On a weekly test in which the time taken to catch each animal was recorded, the indulged beagles became exceedingly shy and wary of being caught when approached by the experimenter or others. We would suggest that the fear which had been experienced first only relatively late in the relationship between the beagle and the experimenter had both an immediate and a delayed action which competed with the positive social affect in contrast to the disciplined beagle where this conflict was attenuated by graded doses of fear arousal and reduction. Why the other socially responsive breed, the wire-haired terrier, did not respond in the same way is not yet known.

We see here an important demonstration of how the affect of joy in response to social stimulation is important in making possible lasting social attachments. Much depends not only on the presence of this affect but on the relative strength of competing affects. If the animal is more fearful than joyous no relationships can be established. If the animal is more excited by the impersonal environment than joyous at social experience, then this also is unfavorable to the development of strong social relationships. Finally, if an otherwise socially oriented animal is suddenly frightened by the one he is attached to and this fear is not habituated, a serious conflict between these two affects may be created with enduring consequences for the maintenance of social relationships.

Further, social responsiveness or preference for the absence of members of one's own species have been selected by animal breeders for different purposes, using the same species at the beginning of selective breeding.

According to Darling,[19] in the hills of Scotland, man has bred out the social characteristics of his sheep. The mountain blackface sheep feeds wide and does not collect in groups of more than five or six. They have marked territorial preferences and individuals of the flock have places on the ground which they like particularly. They have little social system. It was desired to have them feed wide in a mountain country where there are no serious predators and no particular problems in moving them.

In Spain, however, the Merino sheep were known as the "trans-humantes" because they had to make long journeys in large flocks between winter and summer grazings. This flocking instinct is genetic and was fostered for ease and safety on the journeys. They feed over the country as a flock. This characteristic is made use of today where territories are large and have numerous predators.

In order to eat, and not be eaten, most animals must achieve some knowledge of the structure of the world they live in, of who threatens to eat them, and

[19] F. Frazer Darling, *A Herd of Red Deer* (London: Oxford Press, 1937).

The Biopsychosociality of the Family

of who can be eaten and how. According to Romer's[20] theory of chordate evolution, the ancestral types exhibited little behavior except regulation of their feeding apparatus, with almost no "somatic" behavior to external stimuli except protective contracting movements. The elongation of the body and tail and the correlated sense organs and nervous system enabled swimming motions, which, in the beginning, simply brought the feeding mechanism to an appropriate location. The greatest change was that from passive filter feeding to positive food seeking, which took place with the acquisition of jaws. From that point onward, through the stages of higher fish, amphibians, and mammal-like reptiles, the mammal line became a series of primarily aggressive carnivores, mainly eaters of other vertebrates. In support of locomotion, the active pursuit of food and the active dealing with enemies by flight or fight, the affect system assumed more and more importance. To these ends, the affects of interest, startle, fear, and aggression have been evolved through natural selection.

The affect mechanism is in large part an assembly of organs put together by an inherited program which determines how they shall act in concert. For example, all of the organs assembled in panic—the chest, the heart, the face, the blood vessels, the endocrines, the stomach, the brain—also have other non-affective functions. The panic or terror assembly is quite different from other affective assemblies of the same organs, and from the unassembled aggregate of the same organs. Under non-affective assembly the heart, which pounded in fear, may loaf

[20] Alfred Sherwood Romer, "Phylogeny and behavior with special reference to evolution," *Behavior and Evolution*, edited by Anne Roe and George Gaylord Simpson (New Haven: Yale University Press, 1958), pp. 48-75.

along, the stomach continue the digestion of a recent meal, the brain return to its alpha activity, and so on. Each of these organs is involved in numerous good works which engage them in changing assemblies as these are programmed to meet varying contingencies.

Despite the fact that the component organs of an affect assembly may react quite differently when the organism is reacting affectively than when assembled, for sleep, let us say, it is nonetheless true that the characteristic affects of any animal are necessarily influenced by what these organs are designed to do in general. An animal with a somewhat sluggish metabolism could not be expected to become as excited or afraid as an animal who burned the candle of life more brightly, even though for him he was living life to the full.

We are proposing that an animal's way of life and adaptation to his environment must influence the affects he will be capable of emitting. Several years ago Crile[21] proposed that the autonomic and endocrine systems of animals are systematically correlated with the way of life of the animal. In pursuit of this hypothesis he traveled over the world in search of great varieties of animals, measuring and weighing the brain, autonomic and endocrine organs of almost four thousand animals. Crile found evidence that the relative dominance of weight of the heart, thyroid, adrenals, and celiac ganglia were related to each animal's way of life.

He predicted and found evidence that the adrenal gland-celiac ganglion dominance was most marked in the cat family and the rodents in which both attack and defense depend on outburst energy. Among

[21] George Washington Crile, *Intelligence, Power and Personality* (New York: McGraw-Hill, 1941).

the 248 species that Crile and his associates dissected they found the largest and most complex celiac ganglia and plexuses in the lion. He found that the more highly specialized an animal is for a rushing attack, the more the adrenal glands and the celiac ganglia dominate, so that energy may be mobilized quickly. On the other hand, following such a convulsion of activity, there is rapid exhaustion. The cat family in general has no great endurance.

In contrast to explosive energy mobilization mediated by the adrenal gland and celiac ganglia, Crile proposes that constant energy is mobilized by the hormone of the thyroid gland. He expected therefore that in animals adapted to the long chase, either as pursuer or pursued, the adrenal gland-celiac ganglian dominance should be less marked and these animals should have larger hearts and thyroid glands. He examined the dog family, especially the wolf and the impala, and compared the relative weight of heart, brain, adrenal and thyroid organs with those of a member of the cat family of about the same size and weight, the jaguar. As predicted, the dogs had a larger thyroid and smaller adrenal than the jaguar, as well as the larger heart. The adrenal was still slightly larger than the thyroid, whereas in the cat family it is much larger.

Although all dogs that hunt by scent have the wolf pattern of only slight thyroid dominance over the adrenal gland, the greyhound, which runs by sight rather than scent and who is equipped to take his prey through high-speed sprinting in a short rush, has the energy organs of the cat family with its adrenal prominence.

Crile also found the same relationship to hold between the eagle and the vulture. The eagle is individualistic, killing no animal larger than he can eat

154

alone. He must first overtake his prey, then seize and lift it from the ground or capture it in mid-air. Crile suggests that the energy requirements of the eagle are on the order of the cat, whereas those of the vulture are on the order of the long pursuit animals, such as the wolf. The vulture cooperates with other vultures. He soars in the air, spaced apart, and spends little energy for finding his food since the actions of those that are descending serve as the signal to those still in the skies. Since the food it eats is dead and soft, no unusual energy is required to eat it. Crile found that in the eagles the adrenal glands were one and one-half times as large as the thyroid gland following the pattern of the cat family; in the vultures the thyroid glands were nearly equal to the adrenal glands in size, as in the dog family.

In the 500 primates and particularly the anthropoid apes that Crile dissected, he found a larger ratio of brain to body weight than in any other wild or domestic animal of comparable size, but the ratio of thyroid to adrenal gland was not like that in man, but rather had an adrenal dominance. In the chimpanzee the ratio is 2-1 in favor of the adrenal gland. Crile attributes this to the way of life of the primates in the wild state—their tree life. He suggests that one has only to consider the stealthy tree-climbing leopard, the enemy of the primates, to realize that if they had had the thyroid-adrenal balance of man they would have been more intelligent, but too slow to escape the leopard—and would have left no progeny.

In man, the thyroid is relatively larger than in any other land animal and is larger than the adrenal in comparison with the ape and virtually all the wild land animals who have a larger adrenal than thyroid. In the fetus and human infant the adrenal gland is larger than the thyroid. At the time of birth there be-

The Biopsychosociality of the Family

gins a gradual decline of the adrenal gland dominance which continues until the twenty-first year at
which time the thyroid is two and one-half times the
size of the adrenal glands. Crile attributes some of
the volatility of the infant to this early, more primitive endocrine balance.

More recent biochemical and behavioral studies
have confirmed and further illuminated the interdependency between the way of life of the animal and
his energy-controlling systems.

In 1948, Tullar, Tainter and Luduena[22] showed
that in addition to adrenalin the adrenal medulla
secreted another hormone, which they called nor-
adrenalin which has only the effect of stimulating
the contraction of small blood vessels and of increasing the resistance to the flow of blood. Von Euler[23]
found that specific areas of the hypothalamus caused
the adrenal gland to secrete adrenalin, and that other
areas of the hypothalamus cause the adrenal gland
to secrete nor-adrenalin. Euler compared the ratio of
adrenalin and nor-adrenalin secretion in different
wild animals and found that aggressive animals such
as the lion had a relatively high amount of nor-
adrenalin whereas animals such as the rabbit which
depend for survival on flight have relatively high
amounts of adrenalin. Animals both domesticated
and wild that live very social lives, such as the ba-
boon, also have a high ratio of adrenalin to nor-
adrenalin. Hokfelt and West[24] established that in
children the adrenal medulla has more nor-adrenalin

[22] B. F. Tullar, M. L. Tainter, and F. P. Luduena, "Levoar-
terenol," *Science, 107* (2767): 39-40, 1948.

[23] U.S. v. Euler, "A Specific sympathomimetic ergone in
adrenergic nerve fibres (Sympathin) and its relations to
adrenaline and nor-adrenaline," *Acta Physiol. Scand.,* Vol.
12 (1946), pp. 73-97.

[24] See page 248.

Silvan S. Tomkins

but later adrenalin becomes dominant. These more recent biochemical findings are not in conflict with Crile's findings but do add another important dimension to the significance of the adrenalin gland. It would appear that an important differentiation between types of emotion may be based on these biochemical differences within the adrenal gland hormonal secretions.

Richter's[25] study of the domestication of the Norway rat and the effects of selection for docility and laboratory manners on the size of the adrenal gland has supported Crile's report on the atrophy of the adrenal gland in captive lions, and the general covariation of the adrenal with "wildness."

The Norway rat was first brought into the laboratory about the middle of the nineteenth century and has thus been domesticated for over a century for a very restricted way of life. The beauty of Richter's study consists in the present abundance of the wild form so that the selective effects of domestication can readily be determined, by comparing the two animals under the same conditions (although the experimental method inclines more scientists to put the wild rat under "experimental" conditions than to put the tame rat under wild conditions).

Richter reports that some organs do not change at all, some become larger, some become smaller. The organs which become smaller are those which Crile implicated as energy-controlling organs: the adrenals, the liver, heart, preputials, and brain. The adrenals may be one-third to one-tenth as large as in the wild rat; the brain one-tenth to one-eighth smaller. The thymus is larger in the domesticated rat at all

[25] Curt Paul Richter, "Domestication of the Norway rat and its implication for the problems of stress," *Proc. Assn. Res. Nerv. Ment. Dis.*, Vol. 29 (1949), pp. 19-47.

The Biopsychosociality of the Family

ages, as is the pituitary. The thyroid, pancreas, and parathyroids have "doubtfully" smaller weights.

The adrenals, according to Mosier[26] and also Woods,[27] not only become smaller but much less active. Whereas in the wild rat ascorbic acid and cholesterol content of the adrenals cannot be depleted even by severe stress or large amounts of ACTH, in the domesticated rat mild stress or small doses of ACTH deplete the adrenals.

The thyroid, though unchanged in size, is also less active in domesticated rats. Both rats become more active on the running drum during starvation, but the domesticated rats are less active than the wild rats.

Griffiths[28] found that domesticated rats fed on a magnesium-deficient diet developed audiogenic fits, which proved lethal within the first few days. Wild rats developed fewer fits, and none died. Domesticated rats are also more susceptible to poison than are wild rats. They are also more susceptible to middle ear infection. The gonads develop earlier, function with greater regularity and bring about a much greater fertility in the domesticated than in the wild rat, according to Richter.

After adrenalectomy, domesticated rats have a much smaller replacement need. Thus 87 percent of the domesticated rats survived on salt therapy alone,

[26] Harry David Mosier, Jr., "Comparative histological study of the adrenal cortex of the wild and domesticated Norway rat," *Endocrinology*, Vol. 60 (1957), pp. 460-469.

[27] J. W. Woods, "The effects of acute stress and of ACTH upon ascorbic acid and lipid content of the adrenal glands of wild rats," *J. Physiol.*, Vol. 135 (1957), pp. 390-399.

[28] Wm. J. Griffiths, Jr., "Audiogenic fits produced by magnesium deficiency in tame domestic Norway rats and in wild Norway and Alexandrine rats," *Amer. J. Physiol.*, Vol. 149 (1947), pp. 135-141.

only one in fifty of the wild survived. Adding desoxy-corticosterone acetate (by pellet) and cortical extract in addition did not suffice to keep more than a small portion alive. Covian[29] subjected wild adrenalectomized rats given replacement therapy to the stress of fighting. Most of them died within a day or two after the fighting, and in some instances the rats died while fighting even though no observable injuries had been inflicted.

Behaviorally, the domesticated rats are more tractable, less suspicious, and show less tendency to escape than wild rats. When wild rats are placed in a fighting chamber and shocked electrically, they fight with each other, often to the death. The domesticated rats do not fight, but attempt to minimize the shock by jumping into the air or standing on their two hind feet.

Richter speculates that in the beginning of domestication only the tamest of the wild rats mate and give birth to young and only the tamest of these nurse their babies to the weaning stage, since wild rats will kill or eat their litter in response to unexpected sounds. In this way tameness and fertility are favored by the laboratory environment. Since this environment is extremely protective, these animals survive.

King and Donaldson[30] attempted to reproduce the entire domestication process under controlled conditions. They started with six wild rats and bred them

[29] M. R. Covian, "Role of emotional stress in survival of adrenalectomized rats given replacement therapy," *J. Clin. Endocrinol.*, Vol. 9 (1949), p. 678.

[30] H. D. King and H. H. Donaldson, "Life processes and size of the body and organs of the gray Norway rat during 10 generations in captivity," *Am. Anat. Mem.*, Vol. 14 (1929); and "Life processes in gray Norway rats during 14 years in captivity," *Am. Anat. Mem.*, Vol. 17 (1939).

through twenty-five generations. They found that, from one generation to the next, gradual changes in organ weights and behavior occurred that were all in the direction of the present-day domesticated animal, but only at the twenty-fifth generation approached the average levels of the domesticated rats.

First generation captive wild rats grow up to be less suspicious, less fierce, and more tractable than their parents, but they are very nervous, bite readily, and still make use of any opportunity to escape. Their reactions to the self-selection diet are very different from those of their parents. They sample all the substances and grow normally on their selections.

The evidence we have presented from Crile and Richter gives an affirmative answer to the hypothesis with which we began—that an animal's way of life exerts, through natural selection, a profound influence on the nature of the affects he will be capable of emitting. How he gets his food and how he defends himself depend on the structure of his body, which determines both the kind of affect he is able to emit and the kinds of behavior this affect will mediate.

Not only are some animals more aggressive and fearful than others, as Richter has shown, but the specific profile of arousal, maintenance, and decline of the *same* affects, may be of decisive importance, as we can now see from Crile's work. This difference in profile of arousal and maintenance of aggression between the cat and dog family, for example, would appear to be a function of the way the animal stalks its prey. It would seem unlikely that an animal whose aggression is closely coordinated to a sudden rush against its prey would be capable of very graded aggression. Indeed, we know that the "spit" of the cat resembles the profile of a sneeze in its sudden arousal and reduction. The aggression of the dog family, on the other hand, appears to be capable of both a slower and a more graded build-up, and a more sustained arousal. Crile's work permits us to place these fundamental parameters of affect arousal and inertia in a general evolutionary context. Indeed, this more modulated characteristic of the affect system in the dog family may well account for this animal's capacity for general amiability and domestication. Consider the diffuse friendliness of this animal, compared with other animals.

Birds reared by hand, according to Scott,[31] may develop great dependence on humans, but they then become uninterested in their own species and are unable to mate with their own species in captivity. Mallard ducks who become "imprinted" by human beings at an early age soon thereafter develop a fear response which interferes with further imprinting. The dog, also, despite centuries of domestication, is capable of developing somewhat similar fear of man, but there is a marked difference in the possibilities for reduction of this fear.

Scott has reported numerous studies on fear of man in young dogs. Puppies reared in comparative isolation until five weeks of age are afraid of humans at this time. This disappears within the next two weeks, if they are handled often. If they are taken from a litter at three or four weeks and raised by hand, they show no fear at five weeks. If, however, they are allowed to run wild until twelve weeks, they become increasingly afraid of man and almost impossible to catch. If caught and forced into close interaction with a human caretaker and feeder, they can be socialized but remain somewhat afraid of humans and less responsive to them. Despite the fact

[31] John Paul Scott, *op. cit.*

that the dog can also develop fear of man, it is clear that he is more easily domesticated than many other animals, even after the optimal critical period has passed. It is my belief that this is due to the relatively more graded fear and aggression response which the dog is capable of emitting as well as the more sustained positive affects which the dog is capable of emitting. In comparison, the cat (and perhaps the bird) is much less capable of emitting sufficiently graded intensities of fear or aggression to make domestication easy or even always possible.

In addition to a general increase or decrease in emotionality, varying graded and ungraded profiles of arousal, we may note in these reports a persistent correlation between aggressiveness and fearfulness. There is a suggestion in Crile's evidence that this correlation is due to utilization of largely overlapping organ systems. This is particularly marked in the rat, whose change from the wild to the domesticated state reduced *both* timidity and aggressiveness. The horse also clearly becomes both more aggressive and more fearful as he evolves into a race horse. There is much evidence that the cat is capable of both great fear and aggression. There is a persistent line of evidence in Crile that the more reasonable and tractable animals, such as the Arabian horse, the dog, and adult man, have become so through a diminution in the dominance of their adrenal glands over their thyroid. The volatility of the human infant, on the other hand, he attributes to the early dominance of the adrenal over the thyroid gland.

As we have seen, the more recent evidence on adrenalin and nor-adrenalin would argue that differences in the predominance of one hormone or the other would favor predominance of fear or aggression. However, these findings are not inconsistent with the further possibility that the relative predominance of adrenal over thyroid might favor both intense ungraded aggression and fear, and the predominance of thyroid over adrenal favor the more graded control of fear and aggression.

Crile sees the diminution in the dominance of the adrenals as the necessary condition for the development of rationally controlled affect. Richter, on the other hand, sees with alarm the paradigm of modern man in the atrophy of the adrenals in the domesticated rat. He fears that modern man is deteriorating biologically because he has overprotected the weak and helpless and deformed. The price for this, he thinks, will be the same as for the domesticated rat. In the laboratory environment there are now known to be twenty-three strains that survive and reproduce only by virtue of that environment: rats that are toothless, hairless, tailless, wobbly, waltzing, jaundiced, anemic, etc.

One cannot escape the impression that implicit values about aggression and volatility are here involved. For Crile the moderation of this affect combined with the growth of the brain is the glory of man. For Richter it is just this loss of animal vigor which is most alarming. This is perhaps the point at which the implicit Darwinian undercurrent in both theorists needs to be examined.

Animal life, like human life, is not exclusively a matter of tooth and claw. Fundamental as aggression and fear are, they do not exhaust the relevant vital affects either for man or animals. The decline of aggression in modern man and the atrophy of his adrenals, if such should turn out to be his destiny, should not be taken as equivalent to a generalized decline in emotionality and vigor, as Richter suggests. Nor should the dominance of the brain in man be taken as a measure of his sweet reasonableness and his ascendancy. Man is both vigorous and affectful, as well as intelligent. What is missing in the accounts of Richter and Crile are the remaining affects and their biological substrates—the affects which mediate social responsiveness and the affects which mediate curiosity and intelligent behavior.

Social responsiveness is a critical biological characteristic in all animals who are adapted to the presence of their own particular species. While there are species that are severely individualistic, it is also clear that many species, including man, have evolved to be adapted not only to a specific physical habitat but also to a specific social habitat, namely others of their own species. Just as animals vary in the spectrum of the physical environment to which they are adapted, so do they vary in the spectrum of the social environment in which they can function and reproduce themselves. A solitary member of a complex social group like an ant colony is no different essentially than a fish out of water.

One of the conditions which determine that some animals become socially responsive is the reproductive rate of the species. Just as the human infant's long period of biological helplessness requires that he be socially responsive and that he be cared for if he is to survive at all, so certain species must be socially responsive because their low reproductive rate requires a critical minimum population density if the species is to reproduce itself at all.

A small population with a low reproductive rate is vulnerable to sudden storms or environmental changes which may wipe it out. It is also more vulnerable to predators, since animals who are ordinarily socially organized for mutual defense in a large group may be unable to give each other the mutual protection necessary for their survival when there remain only a small number of them.

According to Scott, many of the sea birds lay only one or two eggs a year. They flourish as long as there is a big population. But if the population is much reduced it takes a long time to build up the numbers again and they are in danger of being wiped out entirely. Many species which have become extinct are highly social in nature with low rates of reproduction.

By way of contrast, Scott cites a species like the house mouse as one which survives well, with a high reproductive potential and a low degree of social organization, so that their populations come back readily from small numbers. These may start a new population in a vacant area from a single pregnant female.

Social animals are social in many different ways, for different reasons and by means of different mechanisms. The howling monkey is a highly social animal, not in the sense in which the ant or chicken is, i.e., on rigid social differentiations, but rather by virtue of dominant positive social affects—very little aggression, much concern and sympathy for the young, and much imitation. These monkeys constantly follow each other's movements while they wander about and feed. The mother constantly attends the needs of her young. The older males, although usually indifferent to the young, become very excited if a young monkey falls out of the tree and howls until it is rescued.

The howling monkeys, though they exhibit a great deal of sexual behavior, do not exhibit possessiveness or jealousy. The females are in heat for several days during which they initiate sexual behavior with any available male who stays with the female until sati-

The Biopsychosociality of the Family

ated, at which point the female moves to another male. The relationships are temporary and non-specific.

It is quite possible that it is the rather general lack of aggression which the howling monkeys express toward each other which accounts for this unaggressive sharing of sexual partners.

Leadership is non-hierarchical. The males move through the trees, each one exploring separately, looking for routes through the branches. When one male succeeds he clucks to the others who then follow him. But this leader-follower relationship changes from tree to tree. The males of any particular clan do not fight among themselves, but they roar at any outsider in unison, defending each other, again by imitation and identification. Their generalized imitativeness ranges then from mutual aggressive cries against the outsider, following each other's movements while they wander about and feed, to distress cries of sympathy at the cries of the young.

In contrast to the howling monkeys are social animals whose sociality is based on dominance and submission and on the affects of aggression and fear. It would appear that hierarchical social relationships involving dominance and submission require aggressive and fearful animals. Hens become dominant or submissive as a result of fighting and winning or losing. That fear or distress as well as aggression is probably involved may be inferred from the fact that in the end the dominant hen need only threaten, and a submissive hen moves out of the way.

Scott demonstrated the intimate relationship between aggression and dominance hierarchies by training mice to fight and not to fight.

The fighting of mice can be inhibited by handling

them just before they are put together. By doing this to pairs of animals they were made to live together without fighting for some weeks thereafter. They trained mice to become more aggressive by having them first briefly attacked by other males and repeatedly allowing them to attack helpless mice. When these trained fighters were paired, they fought. Thereafter the winner would chase the loser whenever they met. Whenever fighting was prominent, a dominance hierarchy based on this was formed. When mice lived together without fighting there was no dominance hierarchy established.

The second great class of affects neglected by Crile and Richter are those upon which the development of the intellectual capacities of the animal largely depend. This is the affect of interest, which prompts the exploration of novelty rather than its avoidance in fear, or its destruction in anger. This affect appears to be stronger in some animals than in others, and to vary within strains of the same family.

McClearn,[32] using inbred mice from the Roscoe B. Jackson Memorial Laboratory, has shown clear differences among strains in activity in a variety of novel situations.

Carr and Williams[33] found that in a Y maze, hooded rats showed more exploratory behavior than albino and black rats.

The great curiosity of the cat and the primates has only recently come under experimental scrutiny,

[32] G. E. McClearn, "The genetics of mouse behavior in novel situations," *J. Comp. Physiol. Psychol.,* Vol. 52 (1959), pp. 62-67.

[33] R. M. Carr and C. D. Williams, "Exploratory behavior of three strains of rats," *J. Comp. Physiol. Psychol.,* Vol. 50 (1957), pp. 621-623.

largely because the most curious animal of all, man, was not prepared to believe there was any such motive in animals.

If man can selectively breed other animals for such specific affective and behavioral characteristics as social responsiveness, aggressiveness, individualism, flexibility, emotionality, and maze-running ability, despite his ignorance of the specific genetic factors which are involved, it is certainly possible that natural selection, through differential reproductive success, could also have favored specific affective characteristics in man. It is our belief that such was indeed the case and that natural selection has operated on man to heighten three distinct classes of affect—*affect for the preservation of life, affect for people,* and *affect for novelty.* He is endowed with specific affects to innate activators so, for example, he fears threats to his life, is excited by new information, and smiles with joy at the smile of one of his own species. (The mechanism for this smile, while inevitably leading to joy at the face of the other, seems to be sufficiently complex as to call into question whether one can appropriately refer to the human face as a special releaser. This will be discussed later.) The human being is equipped with innate affective responses which bias him to want to remain alive and to resist death, to want to experience novelty and to resist boredom, to want to communicate, to be close to and in contact with others of his species, to experience sexual excitement and to resist the experience of head and face lowered in shame.

Not only does man possess a broad spectrum of affects, but it would appear that in terms of Crile's analysis, man is capable of both sustained as well as peaked affective response. We should of course expect that the general increase in degree of differentiation of his nervous system should be matched with an increased degree of differentiation in his endocrine system as well as in the striped musculature of his face, both of which would subserve increased complexity of affective expression and experience. Such increased differentiation would permit curiosity, love, aggression, and fear which varied from sudden intense peaked phrases to more moderate, sustained commitment to people, to work, and to self-protection. We should expect, and we do find, that the human animal is also capable of exerting himself for sustained periods with great intensity of affect, for which he will incur a physiological debt.

If this is so, it is clear that his integration of these needs cannot be perfect nor can he be more than imperfectly adapted to his changing environment. There could be no guarantee that selection for social responsiveness might not conflict with selection for self-preservation responsiveness and with selection for curiosity and responsiveness to novelty, and thus complicate the problem of the integration of these characteristics. Nor could multi-dimensional criteria of any kind guarantee adaptation to a changing environment. No animal, of course, is completely adapted, but some animals have been able to attain a closer fit within a narrow niche by combining specialization of characteristics and restriction of movement to an equally specialized environment. In the case of man, natural selection was operating on a broad spectrum of characteristics for adaptation to a broad spectrum of environments.

Let us return to our examination of the nature of the affect system in the human being. The question we will consider is the exact site of the affective responses.

The Biopsychosociality of the Family

THE SITE OF THE AFFECTS

Most contemporary investigators have pursued the inner bodily responses, after the James-Lange theory focused attention on their significance. Important as these undoubtedly are, we regard them as of secondary importance to the expression of emotion through the face. We regard the relationship between the face and the viscera as analogous to that between the fingers and forearm, upper arm, shoulders, and body. The fingers do not "express" what is in the forearm, or shoulder, or trunk. They rather lead than follow the movements in these organs to which they are an extension. Just as the fingers respond both more rapidly and with more precision and complexity than the grosser and slower moving arm to which they are attached, so the face expresses affect, both to others and to the self via feedback, which is more rapid and move complex than any stimulation of which the slower moving visceral organs are capable. There is, further, a division of labor between the face and the inner organs of affective expression similar to that between the fingers and the arm. It is the very gross and slower moving characteristic of the inner organ system which provides the counterpoint for the melody expressed by the facial solo. In short, affect is primarily facial behavior. Secondarily it is bodily behavior, outer skeletal and inner visceral behavior. When we become aware of these facial and/or visceral responses we are aware of our affects. We may respond with these affects, however, without becoming aware of the feedback from them. Finally, we learn to generate, from memory, images of these same responses which we can become aware of with or without repetition of facial, skeletal, or visceral responses.

Silvan S. Tomkins

If we are happy when we smile and sad when we cry, why are we reluctant to agree that this is primarily what it means to be happy or sad? Why should this be regarded as an "expression" of some other, inner state? The reasons are numerous, but not the least of them is a general taboo on sharing this knowledge in interocular intimacy.

The significance of the face in interpersonal relations cannot be exaggerated. The face is particularly critical in the bond which develops between the mother and her child, and we will examine this in some detail presently. At the moment we are more interested in examining its general motivational significance. It is not only a communication center for the sending and receiving of information of all kinds, but because it is the organ of affect expression and communication, it is necessarily brought under strict social control. There are universal taboos on looking too directly into the eyes of the other because of the likelihood of affect contagion, as well as escalation, because of the unwillingness to express affect promiscuously, and because of concern lest others achieve control over the self through knowledge of one's otherwise private feelings. Man is primarily a voyeuristic animal not only because vision is his most informative sense but because the shared interocular interaction is the most intimate relationship possible between human beings, since there is in this way complete mutuality between two selves, each of which simultaneously is aware of the self and the other. Indeed the intimacy of sexual intercourse is ordinarily attenuated, lest it become too intimate, by being performed in the dark. In the psychoanalytic myth, too, the crime of the son is voyeuristic in the primal scene, and Oedipus is punished, in kind, by blindness.

The Biopsychosociality of the Family

The taboo on the shared interocular experience is easily exposed. If I were to ask you to turn around and stare directly into the eyes of the other and permit the other to stare at the same time directly into your eyes, you would become aware of the nature of the taboo. Ordinarily we confront each other by my looking at the bridge of your nose and your looking at my cheek bone. If our eyes should happen to meet directly, the confrontation is minimized by glancing down or away, letting the eyes go slightly out of focus, or attenuating the visual datum by relating it principally to the sound of the other's voice which is made more figural. The taboo is not only a taboo on looking too intimately, but also on exposing the taboo by too obviously avoiding direct confrontation. These two strategies are taught by shaming the child for staring into the eyes of visitors and then shaming the child a second time for hanging his head in shame before the guest.

Only the young or the young in heart are entirely free of the taboo. Those adults whose eyes are caught by the eyes of the other in the shared interocular intimacy may fall in love on such an occasion or, having fallen in love, thereby express the special intimacy they have recaptured from childhood.

THE PRIMARY AFFECTS AND THEIR ACTIVATORS

If the affects are primarily facial responses—what are the major affects? We have distinguished eight innate affects. The positive affects are, first, *interest or excitement,* with eyebrows down, stare fixed, or tracking an object. Second, *enjoyment or joy,* the smiling response. Third, *surprise or startle,* with eyebrows raised and eyeblink. The negative affects are, first, *distress or anguish,* the crying response. Second, *fear or terror,* with eyes frozen open in fixed

172

stare or moving away from the dreaded object to the side, and with skin pale, cold, sweating, trembling, and hair erect. Third, *shame or humiliation,* with eyes and head lowered. Fourth, *contempt or disgust* with the upper lip raised in a sneer. Fifth, *anger or rage,* with a frown, clenched jaw and red face.

If these are innately patterned responses, are there also innate activators of each affect? Inasmuch as we have argued that the affect system is the primary motivational system, it becomes critical to provide a theory of the innate activators of the affect system. Consider the nature of the problem. The innate activators had to include the *drives* as innate activators, but *not be limited* to drives as exclusive activators, since the neonate, for example, must respond with innate fear to any difficulty in breathing, but also be afraid of other objects. Each affect had to be capable of being activated by a *variety* of unlearned stimuli. The child must be able to cry at hunger, loud sounds, as well as a diaper pin stuck in his flesh. Each affect had, therefore, to be activated by some general characteristic of neural stimulation, common to both internal and external stimuli, and not, like a releaser, too specific a stimulus.

Next the activator had to be correlated with biologically useful information. The young child must fear what is dangerous and smile at what is safe. Next the activator had to know the address of the subcortical center at which the appropriate affect program is stored—not unlike the problem of how the ear responds correctly to each tone. Next, some of the activators had not to habituate, whereas others had to be capable of habituation; otherwise a painful stimulus might too soon cease to be distressing and an exciting stimulus never be capable of being let go—like a deer caught by a bright light. These are some of the characteristics which had to be built into the affect mechanism's activation sensitivity. How were all these criteria satisfied? The most economical assumption on which to proceed is to look for communalities among the varieties of characteristics of the innate alternative activators of each affect. This we have done, and we believe it is possible to account for the major phenomena with a few relatively simple assumptions about the general characteristics of the stimuli which innately activate each affect.

We would account for the differences in affect activation by three general variants of a single principle—the density of neural firing or stimulation. By *density* we mean the number of neural firings per unit time. Our theory posits *three discrete classes* of activators of affect, each of which further amplifies the sources which activate them. These are *stimulation increase stimulation level,* and *stimulation decrease*. Thus, there are guaranteed three distinct classes of motives—affects about stimulation which is on the increase, stimulation which maintains a steady level of density, and stimulation which is on the decrease. With respect to density of neural firing or stimulation, then, the human being is equipped for affective arousal for every major contingency. If internal or external sources of neural firing suddenly increase, he will startle, or become afraid, or become interested, depending on the suddenness of increase of stimulation. If internal or external sources of neural firing reach and maintain a high, constant level of stimulation, which deviates in excess of an optimal level of neural firing, he will respond with distress or anger, depending on the level of stimulation. If internal or external sources of neural firing suddenly decrease, he will laugh or smile with enjoyment depending on the suddenness of decrease or

174

stimulation. The general advantage of affective arousal to such a broad spectrum of levels and changes of level of neural firing is to make the individual care about quite different states of affairs in different ways.

It should be noted that according to our views there are both positive and negative affects (startle, fear, interest) activated by stimulation increase, but that only negative affects are activated by a continuing unrelieved level of stimulation (distress, anger), and only positive affects are activated by stimulation decrease (laughter, joy). This latter, in our theory, is the only remnant of the drive or tension reduction theory of reinforcement. Stimulation increase may, in our view, result in punishing or rewarding affect, depending on whether it is a more or less steep gradient and therefore activates fear or interest. A constantly maintained high level of neural stimulation is invariably punishing inasmuch as it activates the cry of distress or anger, depending on how high above optimal levels of stimulation the particular density of neural firing is. A suddenly reduced density of stimulation is invariably rewarding, whether, it should be noted, the stimulation which is reduced is itself positive or negative in quality. Stated another way, such a set of mechanisms guarantees sensitivity to whatever is new, to whatever continues for any extended period of time, and to whatever is ceasing to happen. In Figure 1, we have graphically represented this theory.

STARTLE, FEAR, AND INTEREST

Let us consider first startle, fear, and interest These differ, with respect to activation, only in the rate at which stimulation or neural firing increases.

Startle appears to be activated by a critical rate of

The Biopsychosociality of the Family

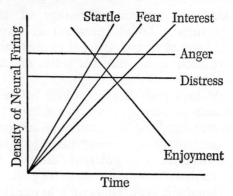

FIGURE 1. *Graphical Representation of a Theory of Innate Activators of Affect.*

increase in the density of neural firing. The difference between startle (or surprise in its weaker form) and interest is a difference in the steepness of the gradient of stimulation. The same stimulus therefore may evoke surprise or interest, depending on the steepness of the rise of stimulation (which in turn depends on numerous factors, prominent among which is the degree of unexpectedness). Thus, a gun shot will evoke startle rather than interest. An unexpected tap on the shoulder by someone who is not seen will also evoke startle rather than interest. In the case of the gun shot, the suddenness of increase of stimulation was primarily in the auditory stimulus itself.

Any auditory stimulus with the physical properties of a square wave might innately activate a startle response. But it should be noted that our theory refers not to the properties of the stimulus but rather to the profile of neural firing. In some cases these will be correlated and in some cases they will not. Otherwise the individual would contrive to be surprised, to be frightened, or to be excited by the same stimulus, no

176

matter how often repeated. Further, the same joke, endlessly repeated, would continue to activate enjoyment and laughter.

The gradients of neural firing must not be exclusively identified with the physical properties of the external stimulus for another reason. Consider the startle response activated by an unexpected tap on the shoulder. Although the suddenness of this stimulus might have been sufficient to activate a startle, certainly the density of neural firing is too low to meet the conditions we have specified. We assume that such a stimulus, by virtue of being unexpected, initiates retrieval of information from memory at a rate sufficient to produce the requisite rate of increase of density of neural firing. This mechanism is most obvious in the "double take." Suppose someone with two heads comes into the room. A cursory scanning of such equipment reveals little out of the ordinary. The man is identified as of the genus *homo sapiens*. But then the information still reverberating in immediate memory leads to a second, much more rapid, search through memory for closer identification and at the same time that the head wheels quickly back into position to have a second look, the combined feedback of these secondary responses triggers a startle response.

The general function of the startle response we take to be that of a circuit breaker or interruptor mechanism, which resets the central assembly. This mechanism is similar in design and function to that in a radio or television network which enables special announcements to interrupt any ongoing program. It is ancillary to every other affect since it orients the individual to turn his attention away from one thing to another. Whether, having been interrupted, the individual will respond with interest, or fear, or joy, or distress, or disgust, or shame or anger will depend on the nature of the interrupting stimulus and on the interpretation given to it. The experience of surprise itself is brief and varies from an essentially neutral quality in its milder form to a somewhat negative quality in its more intense form as the startle response. Whatever its quality, positive or negative, it is frequently confused with the affect which immediately follows it. The surprise of seeing an unexpected love object is an over-all positive experience. The surprise of seeing a dreaded person is an essentially negative experience. In its intense form it is an involuntary massive contraction of the body as a whole which momentarily renders the individual incapable of either continuing whatever he was doing before the startle or of initiating new activity so long as the startle response is emitted.

Our concept of the central assembly refers to the transmuting mechanism (the mechanism that changes messages in the nervous system into conscious form) and those other components of the nervous system which are functionally linked to the transmuting mechanism at a given moment. Without the startle response, information might not be attended to. But the feedback of the startle response is sufficiently sudden and dense to disassemble the ongoing central assembly and to make it possible for the next assembly to be cleared of both the preceding information and the startle feedback, and to include in this next central assembly the components of the nervous system which contain the messages which had activated the startle. Surprise or startle, however, is the perpetually unwelcome competitor to any ongoing central assembly. It does not favor anything and it is against peaceful coexistence with any visitor to consciousness who has outstayed his welcome.

Therefore, as soon as the clamor of the next visitor in the vestibule of the cortex exceeds a critical rate of increase in density of neural firing, the surprise or startle response is activated. Next the central assembly is now cleared of the unwelcome occupant and attends momentarily to that massive, dense feedback from the startle response, which since it is momentary in duration, gives way to the rising, dense neural firing of the messages which had activated the startle. This set of messages then reaches the site of the ongoing central assembly, which is reassembled to include this new information, and this set of messages is simultaneously transformed into the conscious experience of the specific stimulus which gave rise to surprise.

If startle, fear, and interest differ with respect to activation only in the rate at which stimulation or neural firing increases, then we can account for the unstable equilibria which there seems to be between them. First, it would illuminate the familiar sequence of startle, fear, interest. The same object which first startles quickly passes over into fear, and this somewhat less quickly is transformed into interest or excitement. Lorenz[34] has reported the characteristic lability of fear and excitement in the raven, who, on first encountering anything new, flies up to an elevated perch and stares at the object for hours, after which he gradually approaches the object, still showing considerable fear. As he comes closer, he hops sideways with wings poised for immediate flight. Finally, he strikes one blow at the object and flies right back to his perch. This sequence is repeated until eventually he loses interest in it. Harlow

[34] K. Z. Lorenz, "The comparative method in studying innate behavior patterns," *Symposia Soc. Exptl. Biol.*, Vol. 4 (1950), pp. 221-268.

The Biopsychosociality of the Family

and Zimmerman[35] have also noted the alteration between escape from, and exploration of, the feared object when the model mother is present. The infant monkey alternates between clinging to the mother and when the fear has somewhat abated, exploring the object, and then returning to the mother.

Both positive affects—interest and enjoyment—are critical in the development of the infant into a socialized and competent human being. It is the interplay of these two affects which ties the infant first to the mother and then to other human beings. As we will see later, it is possible for interest to be limited to the non-human environment if there is insufficient maternal attention.

With respect to interest or excitement, the latter being the more intense form of the former, while it is sufficiently massive a motive to amplify and make a difference to such an already intense stimulation as that from sexual intercourse, it is also capable of sufficiently graded, flexible innervation and combination to provide a motive matched to the most subtle cognitive capacities. Rapidly varying perception and thinking is thereby combined with varying shades of interest and excitement, which waxes and wanes appropriately with the operation of the analyzer mechanisms. The match between excitement and the drives is a different match from that between excitement and cognition. Because the latter is a process which is much more rapid, and much more variable in time, it necessarily requires a motivational system which is matched in speed, gradation, and flexibility of arousal, combination, and reduction. It must be possible to turn excitement on and off

[35] H. F. Harlow and R. R. Zimmerman, "Affectional responses in the infant monkey," *Science,* Vol. 130 (1959), pp. 421-432.

quickly, to grade its intensity, and above all, to combine it with ever-changing central assemblies. In contrast even with other affects, such as fear and anger, it must have both more and less inertia. It must not necessarily remain activated too long once aroused, but it must also be capable of being sustained indefinitely if the object or activity demands it.

Interest is also a necessary condition for the formation of the perceptual world. In learning to perceive any new object the infant must attack the problem over time. Almost any object is too big a bite to be swallowed whole. If it is swallowed whole it will remain whole until its parts are decomposed, magnified, examined in great detail and reconstructed into a new more differentiated object. There is thus created a variety of problems in early perception. The object must be perceived in some detail, but it must also be perceived in its unity. Attention must steer a middle course between extreme distractibility from one aspect of an object to some other aspect of an adjacent object, and the extreme fixity of a deer caught and immobilized by a light or an animal fascinated by the eyes of a cobra. Attention must stick long enough both to achieve detail and to move on to some other aspect of the object, but not to every competing stimulus in the field. In order to make such graded and differential sampling possible, there must be the continuing support of interest or excitement to the *changing* sampling of the object.

Second, not only must there be a perceptual sampling, but there must also be a sampling of the initially slender inner resources of the infant.

In order to achieve full acquaintance with any object one must vary one's perspectives, perceptual and conceptual. One must look at the object now from one angle, now from another. One must watch the object as it moves about in space. One must switch from a perceptual acquaintance to a conceptual orientation, to remembering it and comparing it now with what it was before. One must also have motor traffic with the object. One must touch it and manipulate it and note what happens to it as one moves it, pushes it, squeezes it, puts it in one's mouth (when one is young), and otherwise produces changes in the object. To the extent to which such manipulation is guided by hypotheses and suggests new hypotheses, one's acquaintance with the object is enriched and deepened.

In order to shift from one perceptual perspective to another, from the perceptual to the motor orientation and back again, from both the perceptual and the motor to the conceptual level and back again, and from one memory to another, one must at the very least maintain a continuing interest in all of these varying transactions with what is the same object. Without such an underlying continuity of motivational support, there could indeed be no creation of a single object with complex perspectives and with some unity in its variety.

The same affect of interest or excitement must be continually reassembled into each succeeding central assembly as the varying commerce with the object disassembles and reassembles both sensory input, memory support, and the varrying transformations on both sets of messages.

DISTRESS

In comparison with startle, fear, and interest, the affect of distress appears to be based not on an increase of density of stimulation, but rather on an absolute level of density of stimulation or neural firing, which deviates in excess of an optimal level of neural firing. Thus pain characteristically produces crying in the infant. The suddenness of pain is not the critical feature of the activation of distress. Either sudden or prolonged pains equally capable of activating distress. Thus, a sudden stab of pain elicits a sudden scream of distress, and prolonged pain ordinarily produces prolonged crying. In contrast to fear, it is the total quantity or density of stimulation over time which elicits crying. It is the quantity rather than the quality of stimulation which appears to be critical. The cry and moan of overly intense sexual pleasure in intercourse is an example of stimulation which is predominantly pleasurable, nonetheless evoking a cry of distress. If distress is activated by a general continuing level of nonoptimal neural stimulation, then we can account for the fact that such a variety of stimuli, from both internal and external sources, can produce the cry of distress in the infant and the muted distress response in the adult. These range from the low level pain of fatigue, hunger, cold, wetness, loud sounds, overly bright lights, to the cry itself as a further stimulus.

The crying response is the first response the human being makes upon being born. The birth cry is a cry of distress. It is not, as Freud supposed, the prototype of anxiety. It is a response of distress at the excessive level of stimulation to which the neonate is suddenly exposed upon being born. Distress-anguish is a fundamental human affect primarily because of the ubiquity of human suffering.

The role of crying in the mother-child relationship is just as critical as the positive affects of excitement and enjoyment. Levy has stressed the attraction between the mother and the infant, but has neglected the critical role of the powerful negative affect of distress.

The general biological function of crying is, first, to communicate to the organism itself and to others that all is not well; second, to do this for a number of alternative distressors; third, to motivate both the self and others to do something to reduce the crying response; fourth, to negatively motivate with a degree of toxicity which is tolerable for both the organism that cries and for the one who hears it cry.

Since the cry is an auditory stimulus, it can be heard by the mother at a distance, which provides a considerable safety factor for the otherwise helpless infant. It is also a much more distinctive stimulus for purposes of communication than are the various thrashing-about movements of which the neonate is capable. It is conceivable that, in the absence of the auditory cry, the human mother would be quite as unable to detect the distress of the neonate as is the chick's mother when she sees but is prevented from hearing the cry. This is also likely because of the number of alternative ways in which the cry can be activated. A mother who could detect distress if a diaper pin were sticking into the infant might be unable to do so if the infant were distressed at being alone, in the absence of a distress cry, since much of the thrashing about of the infant is very similar whether the infant is happy or unhappy.

What the distress cry gains in specificity as a distinctive communication, it somewhat sacrifices because it is a signal of so many possible different distressors. When a mother hears an infant cry, she characteristically does not know what it is crying about. It might be hungry, or cold, or in pain, or lonely. She must try each of these in turn, to find out, and even then the test does not always remove the ambiguity. Since infants will stop crying for many reasons, quite unrelated to what started them, the mother may easily misdiagnose the nature of the distressor. For example, an infant who is hungry may stop crying upon being picked up but start again when it is put down. The mother at this point cannot be sure whether the child is crying from hunger or loneliness.

This degree of ambiguity is a necessary consequence of the generality of activation of the distress response. In lower forms, the cries are more specific in nature. It is an unanswered question how specific the cries of the human neonate may be, although some mothers are confident they can distinguish different types of cries from their infants.

One method of answering such a question would be to record a sample of the cries of a neonate during its first week. Then, at moments when the infant was not crying, subject it to a distributed series of playbacks of its past cries, and record the fresh crying which the infant emitted in response to hearing itself cry. The infant should cry to the sound of its own cry, since the cry is a quite contagious response. One could then examine the degree of correlation between each cry which was used as a stimulus and the contagious response to that cry. If the neonate does emit distinctively different cries, then it might respond differentially to its own distinctive cries; therefore the variance between pairs of cries should exceed that within pairs of cries. To our knowledge such a test method has not yet been employed.

Although the number of alternative activators of the cry creates some ambiguity concerning its significance, it is this multiplicity of activators that makes the cry a response of such general significance. It en-

The Biopsychosociality of the Family

ables general suffering and communication of such suffering. It is as important for the individual to be distressed about many aspects of its life, which continue to overstimulate it, and to communicate this, as it is to be able to become interested in anything which is changing.

Although the communication of distress to the mother is primary during infancy because of the infant's helpless dependency, the significance of communication of distress to the self increases with age. Just as the drive signal is of value in telling the individual when he is hungry and when he should stop eating, so the distress cry is critical in telling the individual himself when he is suffering and when he has stopped suffering. Awareness that all is not well, without actual suffering, is as unlikely as would be the awareness of the threat of a cigarette burning the skin which had no pain receptors. This is to say that, over and above the motivating qualities of pain or of the distress cry, there are important informational characteristics which are a consequence of their intense motivating properties.

The cry not only has information for the self and for others about a variety of matters which need alleviation, but it also motivates the self and others to reduce it. In contrast to fear, which is activated by anything which is so novel that it produces a relatively sharp gradient of density of neural firing midway between what will trigger startle and what will trigger excitement, distress-anguish is a self-punishing response designed to amplify those aspects of the inner or outer world which continue to stimulate neurally with an excessive, non-optimal level of intensity. So long as this non-optimal state continues, the individual will continue to emit the distress cry and suffer the stimulation of this self-

186

punishing response, added to the already non-optimal level of stimulation.

Both the non-optimal level of stimulation and the distress cry may be masked, or reduced, in awareness or in general, by competing stimulation which is more intense and more sharply increasing in intensity and by the affects of startle or fear or excitement which may be activated by such competing stimulation. Despite such competition, the coupling of distress and its activators enjoys the competitive advantage of endurance in its claim upon consciousness. Both the activator and the distress cry are long-term motivators, requiring no novelty to keep the individual under a perpetual bind.

It is because of these very properties that the toxicity of distress had to be kept low if it was to be biologically useful. The problem of toxicity has not received the attention it deserves in the theory of motivation. The problem is a commonplace one in pharmacological therapeutics. Every year hundreds of drugs are discovered to have properties which destroy biological enemies of the human being. These are often valueless in the conquest of disease because their toxicity for the host is as great as it is for the bacteria or virus against which it is effective. The problem was similar in the selection of self-punishing responses for the protection of the organism which was to use them to alarm itself.

If negative affect is too punishing, biologically or psychologically, it may be worse than the alarming situation itself, and it may hinder rather than expedite dealing with it. The evolutionary solution to such a problem was to coordinate the toxicity of the self-punishing response to its duration and to the probable duration of its activator. In the fear or anxiety response, therefore, we are endowed with a transient response of high toxicity, both biological and psychological, and in the distress response we are endowed with a more enduring self-punishing response of lower toxicity.

Fear is a response which, psychologically, is very toxic even in small doses. Fear is an overly compelling persuader designed for emergency motivation of a life-and-death significance. In all animals such a response had the essential biological function of guaranteeing that the preservation of the life of the organism had a priority second to none. The biological price of such a response was high toxicity. Physiological reserves are squandered recklessly under the press of fear, and the magnitude of the physiological debt which is invoked under such duress has only recently been appreciated to its full extent.

Nor has such toxicity restricted to one affect entirely solved the problem. The compelling quality of fear—terror, which in general safeguards the existence of the organism—can lead to its destruction. Occasionally the overly anxious animal is so frozen in fear that he is eaten before he can flee the predator. Particularly in man do we witness excess in both biological and psychological toxicity, of a magnitude that the individual so freezes in fear that he thereby loses his life rather than saves it. Panic may cost an individual his life not only if he freezes, but also if under its duress he surrenders all but the most primitive use of his capacities. For example, many individuals have died in fires because all tried to escape at once and in so doing trampled each other to death. Soldiers in combat have lost their lives in panic, either because they could not pull the trigger of their guns, could not run away, or because they ran wildly into the face of enemy fire.

Despite the toxicity of the fear response, there can

be no doubt of its over-all biological utility so long as it is a transient response and so long as it is activated only by truly emergency situations. It is extremely difficult to make the lower forms suffer chronic anxiety in the way in which it is possible for this to occur in human beings. The development of complex cognitive capacities, in our opinion, made possible the continuous activation of negative affect and required that negative affects be differentiated in terms of toxicity so that less toxic negative affects may be activated. The linkage of high-powered skills of anticipation with massive, overly toxic panic was to make possible both rapid and slow suicide. In the phenomenon of voodoo death, we can see that continuous high-level anxiety sustained for only a few days is sufficient to produce death. Such responses in lower animals are invoked usually only by direct assault or threat of assault.

In man the multiple linkages of such a toxic affect to a variety of internal and external cues makes possible the chronic anxiety neurosis. This disease we believe is a consequence of one of the mistakes of the evolutionary process. The mistake is a mismatch between the arousal of one mechanism which is overly toxic and another mechanism which once aroused is capable of perseverating and sustaining the overly toxic response of the other mechanism. Fortunately the infant is spared this danger of the experience of excessive prolonged anxiety, since its anticipatory skills take considerable time to develop. Secondly, the infant appears to be so sensitive to two other competing affects that the anxiety response is minimized. These are startle and the distress cry. The infant's first reaction to being born is not to become afraid, but to cry; its most common reaction to novelty is not fear, but surprise or another type of sur-

The Biopsychosociality of the Family

prise, the Morro reflex, which is eventually displaced by the startle response. The distress cry is considerably less toxic than the anxiety response and is therefore much better adapted to serve as a self-punishing response (and punishing to others) for long periods of time and to direct attention to activators of prolonged duration.

Thus in the so-called three-month colic the infant may cry more or less continuously the first three months of its life. Although the biological and psychological price of such crying is not trivial, since the baby may become cyanotic, yet its over-all toxicity is sufficiently low so that the infant can survive despite this ordeal. There can be little doubt that three months of panic would place such a severe burden on the infant's physiological reserves that its survival would be extremely unlikely.

There is another aspect to the problem of toxicity which has also received insufficient attention. The crying response has the general biological function not only of communicating to the mother that all is not well with her infant, but also of motivating her to do something about alleviating this distress. This has been achieved by making the sound of the cry a sufficient activator of the distress cry for anyone who hears it. Its sound is within the spectrum of greatest sensitivity of the human ear, and while it does not destroy tissue (so far as we know), it is, along with pain and other types of noise, entirely adequate as a distress activator.

Here again we are faced with a critical toxicity problem. If it is too disturbing to listen to the cry, the infant's life may be endangered, insofar as the mother might either run away from the overly punishing stimulation or become aggressive and hurt the child. Many human mothers do indeed respond to

190

Silvan S. Tomkins

their own distress at hearing their infant cry by essentially abandoning the infant either temporarily until it stops crying, or permanently. Less well known but not uncommon is violence to the point of killing the crying infant or child. In the United States I have noted within the past fifteen years no less than one and sometimes two or three murders each year of an infant or child by a parent or nurse, because the crying of the child could not be tolerated.

Although the distress response itself is not so toxic as this would suggest, it must be remembered that added to the unrelieved distress response are those additional affects which may have been employed in socializing the crying of the parent or nurse. To the extent to which the parent or nurse was made to feel shame, or fear, or anger, or all of these when he or she cried as an infant or child, this burden will usually be reintegrated upon being exposed as an adult to the crying of his or her own or other children.

The combination of the crying of the infant, the adult's own distress, plus other recruited negative affect, is often sufficient to raise the general level of neural firing so that anger is activated. If the crying cannot be stopped, this anger then feeds upon itself until the overt act of violence occurs. One of the most recent incidents of such a kind was in an Associated Press dispatch from Sacramento, California, early in April, 1961: "Donald Mike Johnson, 26, was booked for investigation of murder yesterday after he admitted punching his two-year-old-son to death because the child would not stop crying." Characteristically the parent or nurse has been exposed to several hours of uninterrupted crying, and then has the adult equivalent of a crying tantrum himself.

The problem of toxicity then has not altogether been solved by evolution, even in the case of the dis-

The Biopsychosociality of the Family

tress response, with respect to the punishment of the parents whose care of the infant the cry is designed to evoke. Granting these and other exceptions under particular circumstances, it is generally true that distress is a self-punishing (and punishing to others) response of acceptable toxicity even in intense and prolonged crying, and that fear is much more toxic and therefore tolerable only for very brief periods of time. This increased tolerability of the distress response means that the individual has increased time and degrees of freedom in coping with its alleviation. Obviously, high-intensity distress, or anguish, is more toxic than low-intensity distress; and high-intensity fear, or terror, is less bearable than a low level of anxiety. But for comparable intensities, it is clear that distress is considerably less toxic than fear, and anguish is considerably less toxic than terror.

Fear and terror evoke massive defensive strategies which are as urgent as they are gross and unskilled. Further, they motivate the individual to be as concerned about the re-experience of fear or terror as he is about the activator of fear or terror. In contrast, the lower toxicity of distress permits the individual to mobilize all his resources including those which take time (e.g., thinking through a problem) to solve the problems which activate distress.

Thus if I am distressed at my poor performance as a public speaker, I can usually tolerate this sufficiently to work upon improving my skill. But if I become stage-frightened, I may freeze so that I cannot speak; or so that I then avoid the entire public speaking situation lest I re-experience panic. Again, if failure in work is very distressing, I can try again and succeed. But if failure activates intense fear, of

Silvan S. Tomkins

whatever content (e.g., that I never will succeed, or that I will be punished severely), then if I try again, it is with competence impoverished by the excessive drain on the channel capacity of the central assembly which the toxicity of fear entails.

If I am completely intimidated by fear, then I will not try again, and there is no possibility of solving this particular problem. What is more serious, my development as a general problem solver is thereby jeopardized. Again, if in general social relationships an individual is rebuffed or is left alone and responds with distress, he can re-examine this particular instance, and decide to seek friendship elsewhere, or tolerate the distress of loneliness, or change his own behavior to please the other. If, however, the rebuff or the indifference produces intense fear, the individual may more readily generalize his experience so that there is a withdrawal from interpersonal relationships of any kind; or, in attempting to master such anxiety he may provoke more rejection and then more anxiety because of the grossness, incompetence, and craven submissiveness obvious to those toward whom such overtures are made.

In short, fear is an affect designed to rapidly minimize acquaintance with its source, whereas distress is designed to reduce such acquaintance but with less urgency and therefore with more mobilization of the best resources of the individual, and so with more competence. Under emergency conditions, distress would be a luxury which most organisms could not afford. Only the helpless neonate, who must and is able to call upon the skill of others to survive, can rely exclusively on the distress cry; and only adult human beings who with the aid of their society have managed to cope successfully with the major threats to the physical continuity of life can afford the luxury of primary reliance on the low-toxicity affect of distress.

This is not to imply that distress is not very unpleasant, nor that fear may not be counteracted. Some human beings cannot tolerate distress even in the smallest doses, and some human beings counteract their most intense panic. Upon closer inspection, however, such cases usually show complex affect combinations. Those who cannot tolerate distress most often have in their past suffered great shame, or anger, or fear along with or consequent to distress, which summates with distress. Those who master fear may have in their past also experienced joy in the progressive mastery of negative affect, or do so for the sake of some goal or value whose lure can reduce the affect of fear with a competing affect such as excitement; or finally because to be governed by fear produces shame and self-contempt which is adequate to initiate counteractive behavior which reduces fear. Despite these complications, it remains the case generally that the one affect is much more tolerable, much less toxic *per se,* than the other.

The role of distress in the mother-infant relationship is not limited to motivating the mother to come to the aid of her infant who is in trouble. Paradoxically, there is considerable mutual positive reward to both mother and infant, when, as a result of the mother's intervention the infant suddenly stops crying in distress. The sudden reduction of neural stimulation is an innate activator of the smiling response in both mother and infant. Both are suddenly delighted by the smile to the reduction of distress and the tie between them is thereby strengthened.

The biologically based attraction between mother and child is based both on the mutually rewarding

Silvan S. Tomkins

shared positive affects of excitement and enjoyment, and on the reduction of distress, which is capable of innately activating the rewarding smile of enjoyment in both mother and child. Contrariwise, mothers who permit the infant to cry to exhaustion satisfy neither themselves nor their infants, and as we have seen may even lead to the murder of the infant in the final extremity.

Contrary to Levy's description of the mother-child relationship, such hostility is equally "biological."

ANGER

Anger is the other affect which is activated by the absolute density level of stimulation. It is our assumption that anger is activated by a higher density level of stimulation than is distress. Hence, if a source of stimulation, say pain, is adequate to activate distress and both of these continue unrelieved for any period of time, the combination of stimulation from pain and distress may reach the level necessary to activate anger. This is also why frustration may lead to anger. Further, either distress alone or pain alone might be sufficiently dense to activate anger. Thus, a slap on the face is likely to arouse anger because of the very high density of receptors on the surface of the face. In contrast, a stab of pain elsewere in the body may lack both the requisite density and the duration to activate more than a cry of distress. This principle would also account for the irritability produced by continuous loud noise, which would tend to recruit widespread muscle contraction which, added to the distress affect, could raise the density of stimulation to that necessary for anger. The role of distress and anger in the mother-infant relationship is complex. The infant's crying is capable of innately activating the distress of the mother

195

The Biopsychosociality of the Family

and so enlisting the aid of the mother and strengthening her commitment to her child. But this very combination of the loud crying of distress of the child, plus the evoked distress of the mother is also quite capable of innately activating anger sufficient to attenuate the tie to the infant, and in the extreme case lead the mother to destroy her child.

ENJOYMENT

Finally, in contrast to stimulation increase and stimulation level, there is also the affect which operates on the principle of stimulation reduction. The *smile of joy* is based on such a mechanism.

The smile of joy is innately activated, in our view, by any relatively steep reduction of the density of stimulation and neural firing. Thus, sudden relief from such negative stimulation as pain, or fear, or distress, or aggression, will produce the smile of joy. In the case of pain, fear, and distress, the smile of joy is a smile of relief. In the case of sudden anger reduction it is the smile of triumph. The same principle operates with the sudden reduction of pleasure, as after orgasm or the completion of a good meal, there is often the smile of pleasure. Further, the sudden reduction of positive affect, such as excitement, also activates the smile of joy, in this case usually the smile of recognition or familiarity. In all of these cases it is the steepness of the gradient of stimulation reduction which is critical. A gradual reduction of pain may pass into indifference. A gradual reduction of distress, similarly, may provide no secondary reward of joy. A steep gradient reduction in density of stimulation, necessarily requires a prior level of sufficient density of stimulation so that the requisite change is possible. This means that a re-

Silvan S. Tomkins

duction of weak pain stimulation which is sudden enough may nonetheless not involve a sufficient reduction in density of stimulation to activate the smiling response. Under such conditions whatever reward value there may be in the cessation of pain stimulation is not enhanced by the incremental reward of the smiling response. Further, it means that many familiar objects in the environment may be too familiar to evoke enough even momentary excitement to evoke the smile of joy at the recognition of the familiar and the reduction of very weak interest. In order to enjoy seeing someone or something familiar one must first have been sufficiently interested, so that the sudden reduction of this interest will constitute a sufficient change in density of stimulation to evoke the smiling response.

This theory of the activation of the smiling response enables us to account for phenomena as disparate as the joy of relief from pain and the joy of the infant at the face of the mother. It has been argued that the face of the mother and her smile constitutes a special "releaser" stimulus for the smiling response of the infant. This may indeed be the case, and we will shortly examine the evidence for and against this hypothesis. It is not, however, the only plausible explanation for the ability of the mother's face to evoke the smile of the infant. The alternative which is afforded by our general theory is that the mother's face is one of the few objects in the environment with sufficient variation in appearance and disappearance to produce both excitement at its sudden appearance, and the smile at the sudden reduction of this excitement when the face is recognized as a familiar one. This would account for the smile, observed by other investigators, such as Piaget, at the sudden perception of familiar toys or at somewhat expected and somewhat unexpected "effects" produced by the child's own efforts.

The *second principle* of activation of the smiling response is based upon our theory of memory. Stated most simply, the visual sight of a smiling face can be learned to become a "name," i.e., a message capable of retrieving from memory a specific trace at a specific address. In this case it retrieves the stored memory of how the individual experienced the feedback from the muscles of his own face when he smiled in the past. This retrieved past experience can also become a "name" of a stored program which translates these perceived "awarenesses" into their equivalent motor messages; i.e., a set of impulses which instruct the facial muscles to contract in such a way that the feedback from the contracted facial muscles is equal to the experienced set which initiated this motor translation.

We do not wish at this point to enlarge on subtle distinctions, except to note that the conscious experience of the smile of another face may activate retrieved awareness of one's own past smiles which may then either retrieve a stored program in the manner just indicated *or* directly innervate the innate program of the smiling response via the subcortical centers. The difference in these two routes would be that in the former case a "learned" smile would be activated and in the latter it would be an "unlearned" smile. As in the case of the startle response, the difference between the learned and unlearned version of the same affective response may be so slight as to be indiscriminable to the naked eye, or even when the response is amplified by ultra-rapid moving pictures.

Similarly, we believe one may emit the same, or almost the same, smile through message sets which are learned to be emitted with full conscious intent or through message sets which have been learned as part of another program in consciousness to be retrieved from memory and then to be used to innervate directly the innately organized programs of smiling which are located in subcortical centers. This latter is of course essentially what Pavlov meant by the classical conditioning of reflexes. While the smile is somewhat more complex than a reflex, it is nonetheless innately patterned and capable of being triggered by appropriate subcortical stimulation.

We are attempting here to distinguish learning which utilizes preformed programs from learning and memory which may produce identical responses on a purely learned basis which bypasses the innate programs while it mimics them. It is in part the difference between the "Oh!" of surprise and the same "Oh" of an actor reading his lines. In either event, and by either route, the smile of another person is capable of evoking the smile of the one who sees it, as the yawn is capable of evoking the empathic response. Such mimesis is quite different from the activation by sudden stimulation reduction and somewhat confounds the empirical investigation of the smiling response.

The *third way* in which the smiling response may be activated is through memory or learning. It is not necessarily the case that any experience which produced the smile of enjoyment in the past will be capable of activating the same affect upon being recalled. Emotion remembered in tranquility need to be no more motivating than the toothache which has just stopped aching, which can be recalled with relative calm. Any affect which requires any degree of uncertainty for activation is all but impossible to re-

The Biopsychosociality of the Family

peat exactly, even when the circumstances, in fact or in memory, are duplicated exactly. No joke is ever quite so funny on repetition. Although the smile is an affect which can be emitted to the familiar, it also depends on stimulation reduction, which apart from pain, requires some novelty if excitement is to be activated sufficiently so that its reduction constitutes an adequate stimulus for the smile.

How then is memory or anticipation likely to evoke the smile of enjoyment? Any recollection or anticipation which produces present affect which is sufficiently intense and which is suddenly reduced either through remembered, imagined, or anticipated consequences may evoke the smile of joy. Such would be the case if I anticipated meeting someone who excited me and whom I had not seen for many years. If this generated present excitement the shock of recognition, in visualizing such a reunion, might sufficiently reduce the excitement so that the smile of joy might be evoked. Similarly, if the recollection of such a meeting first arouses excitement which then suddenly is reduced, the smile of joy may be activated in what may be called "postication." If the anticipated or posticipated encounter generates fear, or distress, or shame which is reduced, in imagination, by appropriate counteractive measures, one may smile in joy as a hero. The crushing retort to the insufferable opponent, even when it occurs too late for the battle proper, may bring joy to the heart of the defeated, when one's anger is suddenly reduced by the imagined discomfiture of the adversary. The recollection of past defeat in attempted problem solving, which may occasion present distress or shame, can evoke the smile of joy if suddenly there is an expectation of a solution and with it a rapid reduction of the distress or shame. The same smile of joy may occur in the midst of difficulties if the individual simply imagines himself to have heroically solved the problem. So much for the nature of the activation of the smiling response. We will next examine some of the empirical work on the development of this response.

Smiling has attracted numerous investigators in the hundred years since Darwin first called the attention of psychologists to this response. There were of course many investigators who preceded Darwin, but it was Darwin who first attached a general theoretical significance to the response. Unfortunately a great deal of the empirical research since then has not lent itself to theoretical interpretation, in part because the research was not designed to answer questions of theoretical import. There is no other human affect which has received such intensive scrutiny. Nevertheless, to some extent this is because the response itself is relatively unambiguous, limited in duration and therefore easy to observe.

It seems clear that the smiling response and the mechanism which triggers it are inherited. Whether there is also an inherited receptivity of this mechanism to very particular stimuli, now called "releasers," is less certain.

Sptiz's[36] classic monograph on the development of the smiling response detailed convincingly the potency of the human face and face-like stimuli in eliciting the smiling response. By three months of age, the child will reliably respond to any such stimulus which has two eyes, is presented full face and is in motion, even if the stimulus is a grotesque mask. Only later does the infant learn to respond differentially, by smiling or not smiling, to pleasant and un-

[36] R. A. Spitz and K. M. Wolf, "The Smiling response: a contribution to the ontogenesis of social relations," *Genet. Psychol. Monogr.*, Vol. 34 (1946), pp. 57-125.

pleasant faces or expressions, and to familiar and unfamiliar faces. This evidence obviously suggests that the human face is an innate "releaser" of the smiling response and of the affect of joy. But additional data raise some questions about such a conclusion.

The inherited motor program is probably completed by the twenty-eighth week of gestation in view of the evidence that smiling has been observed in such prematures. Before the smiling response is reliably evoked by specific facial stimulation, it appears to be evoked by numerous and very general aspects of stimulation, external and internal.

Wolff [37] reports on the behavior of four newborn infants he observed twenty-four hours at a time that spontaneous smiling (defined as a slow, gentle, sideward and upward pull of the mouth, without rhythmical mouthing movements or contraction of other facial muscles) was observed after the first twenty-four hours in all four infants. Gesell [38] has also observed a smile in premature babies twenty-eight weeks old, and, as Ambrose has suggested, the smile may occur in utero.

In the first weeks of life smiles are fleeting and sometimes only partial. Some investigators have reported that the smiling response is evoked by nonspecific intense stimulation, whereas others have reported that it is evoked by moderate stimulation. The smiling response to the face generally first appears between the fourth and eighth week.

[37] Peter Wolff, "Observations on the early development of smiling," in B. M. Foss (ed.) *Determinants of Infant Behavior* (New York: John Wiley & Sons, 1961), II, 113.

[38] Gesell, "The ontogenesis of infant behavior," in L. Carmichael (ed.) *Manual of Child Psychology* (New York: John Wiley & Sons, 1946).

Silvan S. Tomkins

Although the smile appears as an organized response before birth, its delayed appearance to specific stimuli depends primarily, it would seem, on the delayed development of visual perception.

Gesell has reported that visual fixation is achieved by about the fourth week. There is by this time sufficient skill for the infant to move his head and eyes within a small arc to follow the moving face of the parent as well as to fixate the non-moving face. The first specific stimulus to which the infant will smile, Ambrose[39] suggests, is anything which is small and has figural qualities. Ahrens found that small, sharply demarcated dots on a card were even more effective in evoking the smile than the whole human face. He found that the number of spots on the card were unimportant as long as the infant's eyes did not move but fixated, and that smiling could at first be elicited by one spot only. The fact that both the shape of the dots and the shape of the card were irrelevant, Ambrose suggests, strengthens his hypothesis that the earliest specific visual stimulus to the smile is figural contrast with a ground.

Kaila[40] observed seventy infants living in institutions for varying periods between the ages of two and seven months. He records that, by three months of age, the interest in the face has become so strong that the use of other visual stimuli is almost impossible.

He used two dark blue glass balls placed as eyes in rectangular openings in a box through which he could see the infants without being seen. Two- and three-month infants did not look at the balls directly but at a middle position equivalent to the top of the

[39] J. A. Ambrose, "The Smiling Response" (Unpublished doctoral dissertation, University of London, 1961).

[40] E. Kaila, cited in Ambrose, *op. cit.*

The Biopsychosociality of the Family

nose. If he reduced the distance between the eyes by half, the infants then looked repeatedly from one to the other. He concluded that what fascinates the infant is not the eyes as such but the gestalt of the eye part of the face turned directly towards him.

He also found further evidence for this assumption in another experiment in which he first looked at an infant directly with his own face, then turned his face to one side, then back to the full-face position. Infants who smiled at the full face stopped as the face was turned to the side, and the smile reappeared as it turned back. This effect was not obtained, however, before three months.

The second important characteristic of the earliest visual stimulus to the smile, according to Ambrose[41] and others, is movement. Ahrens[42] states that movement is sometimes necessary. Spitz and Ambrose report that, as soon as responsive smiling begins, movement is a necessary property until fourteen weeks.

Ahrens has shown that the stimuli which evoke the smile change as the infant develops. At two months, two horizontal black spots are sufficient. It is only in the second month, according to Ahrens, that the horizontal position of the eyes first becomes operative. Coordinated eye movements are not achieved till then, so that the infant is able to look from one eye to the other. His evidence for this is that two spots turned from the vertical to the hori-

[41] J. A. Ambrose, "The development of the smiling response in early infancy," in B. M. Foss (ed.), *Determinants of Infant Behavior* (New York: John Wiley & Sons, 1961), 1, 179-196.

[42] R. Ahrens, "Beitrag zur Entwicklung des Physiognomie- und Mimikerkennens," Z. *fur experimentelle und angewandte Psychologie*, Vol. 2 (3) (1954), pp. 412-454.

zontal position usually evoked smiling but not when turned back again. Up to two months he found that the dots were more effective as a stimulus to the smile than the whole face. Subsequently they ceased to be as effective.

Later in the second month something more similar to the human eye configuration is necessary but the lower half of the face is not. In the third month mouth movements are noticed but only fleetingly. By the fourth month the eye configuration is much more differentiated. It is still a sufficient condition to evoke the smile, but by this time mouth movements, especially widening, are also sufficient to evoke the smile. Head movement intensifies smiling and the general shape of the rest of the body becomes necessary. The expression of smiling plays no role as stimulus up to about five months. A smiling mask was no more effective than a mask with an indifferent expression. In two- and three-month infants a smiling mask with the lower half removed was as effective as one with the lower half smiling. By the fourth month some infants began to turn away from a mask without the lower half of the face.

Between three and seven months the widening of the mouth became more and more effective as a stimulus to evoke smiling. In contrast, infants up to three months do not smile in response to the mouth, not because they cannot perceive it but because when it is motionless it is not enough to draw the infant's attention away from the eyes. Up to three months the infant might pay attention to the moving mouth, but not smile at it.

By five or six months the mask is less effective than the face and often fails to evoke smiling. By the sixth month the eye configuration alone ceases to be

The Biopsychosociality of the Family

a sufficient evoker of the smile. Mouth movements are also necessary. However, the adult is still not recognized as a specific person.

By the seventh month specific individuals began to be recognized and specific expressions responded to differentially.

According to Spitz, in the first six months the infant smiles indiscriminately at every adult offering the appropriate stimulation, whereas in the second six it may smile at one person or another, if so inclined, but will not smile indiscriminately at everybody.

Ahrens reports that infants over five months respond to strangeness either by startle, attentive observation, or turning away their heads. The infant may combine negative affect, wrinkling the forehead, with interest; or it may alternate by hiding its eyes, by turning away and peering furtively again at the face.

From twenty to about thirty weeks there is a maintenance or increase of smiling time to familiar faces and a reduction of response to unfamiliar faces.

According to Ambrose, working with children in institutions, this reduction in smiling to unfamiliar faces takes place gradually. By thirty weeks there is no smiling to unfamiliar faces in most of the infants studied by Ambrose. According to him the duration of smiling to a stranger reaches first its maximum and then its minimum much earlier in infants maintaining a relationship with their mothers at home than in infants who have many relationships, as in an institution. He reports that Bernstein found, with infants living with their mother at home, that sixteen weeks is the equivalent age at which no smiling occurs to an unfamiliar face in most children.

The face which is strange need not be simply that

206

Silvan S. Tomkins

of a stranger. An angry expression of an otherwise familiar face might, Ambrose suggests, also have the property of strangeness.

Ambrose reports further unpublished findings by Bernstein that infants with a good relationship with their mothers eventually show much stronger smiling to strangers, after thirty weeks of age, than do infants having a poor relationship with their mothers. Smiling at strangers is eventually resumed, presumably due to generalization from the mother in these cases.

Ambrose has suggested that the two to seven month period is one of special sensitivity in the direction of learning rather than just one of special opportunity. There has been some evidence favoring such a possibility of a critical period in species other than man.

Jaynes[43] has presented evidence for "latent imprinting." When during the critical period a bird is exposed to a particular object which was not then followed, nevertheless when opportunity to follow is provided after the critical period this results in following only this object. This was not true for a control group which was not exposed early.

Harlow and Zimmerman[44] have reported that monkeys denied physical contact with other monkeys or a mother surrogate until eight months of age develop a less intense and less persistent attachment to a cloth-mother than monkeys raised with a cloth-mother from birth. At nine months of age they spent about half as much time with her and found less reassurance from her when placed in a strange situa-

[43] J. Jaynes, Imprinting: the interaction of learned and innate behavior: II. The critical period, *Journal of Comparative and Physiological Psychology*, Vol. 50 (1957), pp. 6-10.

[44] H. F. Harlow and R. R. Zimmerman, *op. cit.*

tion than did monkeys raised from the cloth-mother from birth. After they were again separated from the cloth-mother for eighteen months, they rapidly lost their responsiveness to her, in marked contrast with the other group which showed overattachment to their cloth-mothers. Further, neither group of monkeys were able, as adults, to form stable attachments to real monkeys nor were they able to reproduce themselves.

When there is an imprinting mechanism, the critical period hypothesis is very compelling since there is evidence that, as in the examples above, if the animal is not imprinted within a particular time period, it is unlikely he may ever be imprinted. If there is no imprinting mechanism involved, it is much less critical when particular experiences occur, yet the cumulative effect of deprivation over particular early periods of development may be equally severe. As we shall see later, one way of producing an autistic child is to severely limit his interpersonal interactions and particularly his smiling interactions.

Whether or not there is a critical period for the smiling interaction with respect to later personality development, there is abundant evidence that interpersonal interaction is at least one of the primary stimuli to the smiling response and that the frequency and duration of smiling depend in part on continuing human stimulation but not on drive reduction in the usual sense.

In one of the earlier studies designed to reveal the basis of the smiling response, Dennis[45] reared babies in such a way that there was minimal exposure to the human face, in particular that feeding and other

[45] W. Dennis, "An experimental test of two theories of social smiling in infants," *J. Soc. Psychol.*, Vol. 6 (1935), pp. 214-223.

care was not accompanied by exposure to the face or voice of the mother. These babies still smiled at the human face and no other stimulus was so effective. He had expected to find evidence for an unconditioned stimulus for the smiling response to which the human face might have become conditioned.

In a more recent experiment by Brackbill,[46] infants who had just eaten to satiety and were freshly diapered, as well as being rested from recent sleep, were subjected to the following stimulation immediately after smiling: the experimenter smiled back, talked, picked up, held, jostled, and patted the infant for 45 seconds and then put him down again. Each conditioning period was for five minutes. This procedure was repeated with intervals varying up to several hours. One consequence was to increase the rate of smiling significantly. Later when no more stimulation of this kind was given the smiling rate declined, eventually to no smiling at all.

This stimulation was visual, auditory, tactile, and kinesthetic. It involved no drive reduction. Here we see that human stimulation is sufficient for evoking the smile and that variations in such stimulation produce concomitant variation in the amount of smiling of the infant.

According to Ambrose there are three places in the sequence of social interplay where smiling is evoked in infants. First, he usually starts to smile when he first sees his mother. Further stimulation at this point by movement, vocalization, or touching the infant usually increases the smiling. Second, if the infant is picked up, held, and spoken to, there is usually some smiling but at less intensity. Third,

[46] Y. Brackbill, "Extinction of the smiling response in infants as a function of reinforcement schedule," *Child Development,* Vol. 29 (1959), pp. 115-124.

subsequent to being picked up and held, further stimulation may result in the re-occurrence of smiling, and when this stimulation is intense, smiling may turn into laughing.

Ambrose asked several nurses to watch for the first time the infants smiled in response to them and to note the circumstances. In each of seven cases the baby was not only looking at the nurse's face, but being held by her either on her lap or on her knee, and being spoken to, which also included her making gentle head movements. These situations arose only after a feeding and the smile appeared only after some minutes. Since these latter conditions are not sufficient, alone, to evoke smiling, Ambrose suggests they play a role of facilitation.

Although it is clear that the motor program for smiling is innate, we are not persuaded that the smile is innately "released" specifically by the human face or by the human smile. It is clear that even if the face is a sufficient condition for activating the smile, it is certainly not a necessary condition. The smile has been observed in prematures, in neonates within twenty-four hours after birth, and in response to numerous internal and external stimuli, and particularly, as Piaget[47] reported, in response to the sudden reappearance of familiar toys.

Piaget observed his own children and reported the conditions under which smiling occurred. In the second and third month he found that his children smiled at inanimate objects as well as their parents and that an essential condition seemed to be the familiarity of objects or people. Piaget suggests that when familiar objects reappear suddenly they release affect, or when a situation is repeated the smile may

[47] J. Piaget, *The Origins of Intelligence in Children* (New York: International Universities Press, 1952).

Silvan S. Tomkins

be released. Only gradually do people monopolize the smile because they are the objects most likely to reappear frequently. The fact that the human face and smile do most frequently stimulate the smile in the infant has been established beyond doubt. We are calling into question only whether this is the consequence of an innate releaser. We are not questioning the innateness of the response itself.

Ahrens has shown that the first stimulus sufficient to evoke a smile is two horizontal black spots on a card, the shape of the dots and the shape of the card being irrelevant. As Ambrose has suggested, anything small with figural qualities seems to be a sufficient stimulus.

If at first it is simply the figural quality of a stimulus, such as a dot on a card, which will evoke the smile, as time goes on there are a great number of changes in the apparent specificity and complexity of the stimulus necessary to evoke the smile. The simplest way of accounting for these changes is in terms of the progressive increase in perceptual and cognitive skill of the developing infant. If the stimulus to the smile is, as we think, a specific gradient of reduction of neural firing, as, e.g., in the reduction of interest, then the smile may be expected to change as the object which the developing child can perceive grows more specific and more complex. As his ability first to be excited by a perceived object and then to recognize it as familiar object increases, we may expect the apparent stimulus to the smile to change as this ability does.

An infant can smile at a couple of dots on a card because this is as complex a stimulus as he can both perceive and in a moment recognize as the same object and hence familiar. This memory is at first a very short-term memory, and this is why the infant

The Biopsychosociality of the Family

rarely smiles immediately at an object, since it takes time for him to first construct it and then to reconstruct it as the same object.

Before he can fixate and coordinate his eyes very well, he is likely to require motion in the object before he can see it and then see it again. As we have seen, motion of the object as a necessary condition of the smile ceases to be such as soon as there is sufficient maturation of the nervous system for the infant to coordinate his eyes so that he can both fixate on an object and also move his eyes to see it in different perspective. For the same reason the smile is rarely immediate in infancy. Ambrose reports that in 70 percent of the infants who smiled at all, the latency of the smile was three seconds or more. Very striking evidence of the tenuous hold which the infant has of even the most familiar object is the sudden cessation of a smile when the face is turned sideways, and the somewhat delayed smile of recognition when it is turned back again to be presented full face to the infant.

Although it takes time for objects to be recognized as familiar, it takes less and less time with continuing exposure to the same stimulus even for infants. Interest in the continuously exposed stimulus declines until there is no possibility of a smile.

Ambrose reported that with most infants smiling usually takes place at the beginning of the appearance of the face of the experimenter, dies out after a short time, usually within the first thirty seconds if not much earlier, and does not occur again however long the experimenter confronts the infant. Within thirty seconds there are usually two or three smiles, the range being from one to six, with a total duration of about five to ten seconds.

Silvan S. Tomkins

The dependency of the smile on interest is shown by the fact that after smiling at the experimeter had waned, the infant would smile if a different person came into the room. Also, a change of simulation in the second half of each run, e.g., by reducing the distance of stimulation, increased the amount of smiling compared with a control group.

Ambrose has also shown that the time during which an infant will smile to a face decreases with the number of times this face is presented, so that after twelve presentations smiling occurred for zero time.

As we should also expect if the smile depends on both interest and reduction of interest through recognition of the familiar, more and more of the face becomes necessary to evoke the smile. Whereas at first two horizontal dots are sufficient, then a human eye-like configuration is sufficient, then some mouth movements and head movements are also necessary in addition to the eyes until finally the whole face is necessary.

Not only is more and more of the face a necessary part of the stimulus to the smile as perceptual and memory skill increases, but the specificity of face which is necessary to evoke the smile also increases at the same time. Eventually, as we have seen, the face of the stranger evokes startle, fear, or interest, but since interest is now no longer reduced by familiarity, there is no smile to the stranger.

Smiling creates a *felicité a deux* similar to and also different from that created by the enjoyment of sexual intercourse. In sexual intercourse the behavior of each is a sufficient condition for the pleasure of each individual for himself and at the same time for the pleasure of the other. This dyadic interaction is inherently social inasmuch as the satisfaction of the self is at the same time the satisfaction of the other.

In the smiling response, as we see it first between the mother and her child, there is a similar mutuality, except that it is on the affect level rather than through mutual drive satisfaction, and it operates at a distance rather than requiring body contact. The difference in this respect is as profound a change in the structure of motivation as was involved in the development of perception with the appearance of distance receptors compared with proximity receptors.

Since the infant will smile at the face of the mother and thereby reward itself, and since the mother will in turn smile at the smile of the infant and thereby reward herself, concurrent smiling is mutually rewarding from the outset. Later, when the child's development is sufficiently advanced, both parties to this mutual enjoyment are further rewarded by the awareness that this enjoyment is shared enjoyment. This is mediated through the eyes. Through inter-ocular interaction both parties become aware of each other's enjoyment and of the very fact of communion and mutuality. Indeed, one of the prime ways in later life that the adult will recapture this type of communion is when he smiles at another person and that one smiles at him and at the same time the eyes of each are arrested in a stare at the eyes of the other. Under these conditions one person can "fall in love with" another person. The power of this dyadic posture is a derivative of an earlier unashamed fascination-and-joy smile. The power of the earlier experience is essentially innate: the match between the stimulus characteristics of the human face and the conditions necessary for innately arousing the reciprocal affects of interest and joy biologically equips the infant, no less than the mother, to be joyous in this way.

More often than not, mutual awareness of each other's smile will include visual awareness of the other's face, including the smile but without high density of conscious reports as compared with visual messages, about the eye of the other. He may look at the other's eyes, but with limited awareness. Because socialization ordinarily places restrictions on the direct intent stare into the eye of the other, adult communion ordinarily excludes prolonged inter-ocular interaction as being excessively intimate. Despite this exclusion there is a deeply rewarding sense of communion made possible by mutual awareness of each other's face in mutual smiling. Awareness of mutuality is achieved without inter-ocular interaction even though this exclusion somewhat attenuates the intimacy of this experience.

The general biological significance of social responsiveness and therefore of any affect which supported such characteristics is manifold. First, since the human infant is the most helpless of animals, it is important that he attract the care of the mother. This is guaranteed first by the distress cry which creates an *infelicité a deux* and prompts the mother to attend to the punishment the infant is experiencing, since the cry as heard will activate the cry in anyone who hears it. It is as unpleasant to hear, as the stimulus which activates it in the infant. In addition to the cry as a motive urging both the infant and the mother to *do* something, there is the positive reward of the shared smile which will make it more likely that, after the crisis signaled by the cry is past, the mother will continue to interact with and stimulate the child. Since the infant must learn how to become a human being from other human beings, his devel-

The Biopsychosociality of the Family

opment necessarily requires much interaction which must begin relatively early with the mother. For this to happen, and to be frequently repeated, both parties must be continually rewarded by each other's presence.

Second, mutual social responsiveness between mother and child not only helps guarantee the survival of an otherwise relatively helpless animal but also makes possible the continuing reproduction of the species.

Social responsiveness in animals is of course by no means a necessary condition of the reproducibility of a species. Yet in some species of animals social responsiveness is one of the techniques by which the group resists extinction. Animals who require cooperation in order to cope successfully with predators, animals with a low reproductive rate, animals whose infants are relatively helpless for a protracted developmental period, and especially animals whose development depends heavily on learning from each other will require motivational systems which punish alienation and isolation. Every consideration which is critical in guaranteeing that the infant survive to reproduce himself is necessary for the preservation of the species, but the latter also requires, over and above individual survival, group competence in dealings with predators, with scarcity of food, with disruption of the group by individualistic motives, and in dealing with a low reproductive rate. Man is one of those animals whose individual survival and group reproduction rests heavily on social responsiveness, and the mutual enjoyment of each other's presence is one of the most important ways in which social interaction is rewarded and perpetuated.

The smiling response and the enjoyment of its feedback, and the feedback of concurrent autonomic and hypothalamic responses make possible a kind of social responsiveness in man which is relatively free of drive satisfaction, of body site specificity of stimulation, and of specific motor responses other than that of the smile itself.

Let us consider the contribution of a social affect to the nature of social ties as compared with the contribution of drive satisfaction to the formation and maintenance of social ties. Freud more than any other theorist tried to account for man's social nature on the basis of the rewards and punishments granted and withheld in connection with hunger and sexuality. It cannot be doubted that the mother, or anyone else capable of granting or withholding either food or sexual pleasure, will necessarily loom large in the life space of any child so influenced. Upon the concept of orality there has been erected in psychoanalytic theory a superstructure of monolithic proportion. Every variety of social responsiveness from passive dependence, through active incorporative behavior, overpossessiveness, oral optimism or pessimism to biting aggressiveness has been regarded as a derivative of the act of sucking or biting and swallowing. Similarly the sexual impulse has been offered as the primary model not only for the family romance but for a variety of other phenomena, ranging from the formation of conscience, through projection into all later authority relationships, to general social cohesiveness.

Freud was not without some misgivings about erecting such a superstructure on the basis of hunger and sexuality. He saw clearly that the waxing and waning of these drives, if accompanied by a concurrent rise and fall of interest in other human beings, could not provide sufficient continuity for minimal social cohesiveness. He solved this problem by postulating that the observed steadier social responsiveness was a somewhat attenuated derivative of the underlying drives.

Homosexuality apart, the sexual drive, insofar as it sensitizes the individual to opposite members of the species, is indeed a powerful amplifier of heterosexual social responsiveness. Nonetheless it would not in and of itself provide sufficient or enduring enough interest in others to produce the social sensitivity characteristic of man. The same would appear to be the case with animals other than man. According to Scott,[48] a lamb reared in isolation will mate and produce young but will ignore other sheep for the rest of its life. The sexual drive is too specific to recruit interest in other sheep except in the service of immediate and direct sexual aims. Such drive specificity is much more characteristic of lower animals than of man and we do not base our case for man on such evidence. Man is much more continuously "ready" for sexual experience, much more excitable by possibilities, evoked either by the presence of potential sexual partners or by erotic fantasies. Despite this amplification of the drive by cognitive and affective elaboration, man's social responsiveness would be quite attenuated if it were based exclusively on the promise of sexual satisfaction or on the threat of its frustration.

In the case of hunger there is no doubt, under conditions of scarcity as it is experienced in many primitive societies, e.g., in the far North or during famine, that almost the entire behavior of man can be understood in terms of an oral complex—the fear and distress of starvation and the excitement and joy in finding and eating food. The hunger drive under such conditions becomes monopolistic not simply be-

[48] John Paul Scott, *op. cit.*

Silvan S. Tomkins

cause one is very hungry but because intense positive and negative affect is combined with the hunger drive and both of these become the focus of phantasy, of planning, and of sustained effort to satisfy the drive and avoid starvation. This is truly an oral complex, but it is also more than a simple oral drive phenomenon.

Since an infant is also in perpetual danger of starvation, it was a simple but important step to scrutinize the oral complex in infancy and its generalization from there to adulthood. There can be no doubt that the psychoanalytic discovery and exploration of the consequences of early oral satisfaction and deprivation for later interpersonal relations and personality development was a revolutionary insight of a creative genius. Pathological phenomena such as the delusions of being poisoned, fears of being devoured, fears of starvation, compulsive overeating, the equally compelling inhibition of eating to the point of death in anorexia nervosa, and many others could now be understood in terms of the oral interactions between mother and child in earliest infancy.

Although not all oral behavior is causally connected with the hunger drive, any more than alcoholism is necessarily connected with thirst, nonetheless some important social needs, some dependence and love, may be uniquely related to early feeding experiences. We regard it as still an open question just how significant the vicissitudes of the hunger drive *per se* will prove to be for understanding personality development. We are not urging that this hard-won insight be lightly surrendered. We are urging, however, that such concepts as the oral stage and the oral character exaggerate the contribution of the hunger drive to personality development while minimizing, even in the oral complex, the impor-

The Biopsychosociality of the Family

tance of non-nutritive oral activity and the associated affective and cognitive components of oral and hunger needs. Further, the preoccupation with the hunger drive has retarded the appreciation of the other biological substrates of the social responsiveness in man and other animals. If, in order to understand a schizophrenic's delusion of being poisoned, we must invoke the vicissitudes of the early oral and hunger experiences, we will have to understand the function of the eye area of the face of the other as an activator of affect to understand the delusion of being watched as well as the depressive's misery at not being watched.

Harlow[49] has shown, in a brilliant series of experiments, that clinging to, and body contact with, a pneumatic, inanimate surrogate mother makes orphaned baby monkeys develop a strong and persistent attachment.

He contrived two surrogate mother monkeys. One was a bare welded-wire cylindrical form with a wooden head and a crude face. The other was similar but was cushioned by a sheathing of terry-cloth. Eight newborn monkeys were placed in individual cages each having equal access to the cloth and to the wire mother. Four received their milk from one mother and four received their milk from the other. In each case this was from a bottle protruding from the general area of the breast of the synthetic mother. The two mothers were physiologically equivalent insofar as the two groups drank about the same amount of milk and gained weight at the same rate. However, psychologically, these two synthetic

[49] Harry F. Harlow, "Behavioral Approaches to Psychiatric Theory," in Jules H. Masserman (ed.), *Science and Psychoanalysis*, Vol. VII, *Development and Research* (New York: Grune & Stratton, 1964), pp. 93-113.

mothers were not at all equivalent. Both groups of monkeys spent much more of their time climbing on and clinging to the terry-cloth covered mother than on the bare wire mother. Those monkeys that were fed by the wire mother spent no more time on her than feeding required. Thus, Harlow argues, and we would agree, affection is not a secondary drive learned from the satisfaction of the primary drive of hunger, but rather is decisively dependent, in this species, on contact comfort.

Harlow then tested the strength of this attachment in yet another way. The infant monkey was exposed to strange objects such as a mechanical teddy bear which moved forward while beating a drum which was calculated to, and which did, frighten the infant monkeys. No matter which mother had fed them, they overwhelmingly sought succor from the terry-cloth mother. This preference was enhanced with the passage of time and increasing experience. In the beginning of the series of experiments the infant might rush blindly to the wire mother, but even if this happened, the infant would soon abandon her for the cloth mother.

Two other factors, motion stimulation and the clinging response, also appear to play a role, although according to Harlow's findings, body contact plays the primary role in the attachment of the infant monkey to the surrogate mother.

Preliminary experiments by Harlow in which monkeys are raised either on the standard cloth mother or on a flat inclined plane tightly covered with the same type of cloth indicate that clinging contact produces a stronger tie than contact per se. Both of these objects permit contact with the soft cloth, but the shape of the mother maximizes clinging and the shape of the plane minimizes it. The monkeys prefer the mother to whom they can cling.

Harlow also investigated the role of motion stimulation in the affection of monkeys. He compared the responsiveness of infant monkeys to two cloth mothers, one stationary and one rocking. All preferred the rocking mother, although there was much daily variability, and variability between monkeys, in this regard. It would seem to increase the affection but not as much as contact per se.

Although the infant monkey is clearly dependent on body contact for it to enjoy and love its mother, and although the same is probably true to some extent for the human infant, it is also clear that if this were to continue to be a necessary condition for affection, it would constitute a severe restriction on the kinds of social responsiveness possible between mother and child, and later between adults. There is, however, evidence from these same experiments that the visible presence of the surrogate mother, without benefit of body contact, begins in infancy to offer some of the same reward as body contact.

The independence of the joy affect from the clinging response and body contact was shown in an experiment by Harlow in which the surrogate mother of the infant monkey was placed in the center of the room and covered with a clear Plexiglas box. These animals were initially disturbed by this, but after several violent collisions with the plastic box, several infants began to be much more active than they were when the mother was available for direct contact. In part this is probably a consequence of competition between the positive affect of interest in the new objects in the room, and the positive affect of joy in clinging to the mother. But there is other evidence that although joy is not as intense under these conditions as when the infant monkey can cling to the mother, yet her visible presence can make a difference. When exposed to a frightening stimulus, fear was most reduced by contact with the mother but also reduced by her visible presence. Under such conditions the infant would be most reassured by contact, next by the sight of the mother, and not at all when the mother was not available visually or by contact.

In what ways is man's social responsiveness different, by virtue of the smiling response, from what it would be if it were exclusively a function of the hunger and sex drives? First of all, a radical increase or decrease in social responsiveness is made possible by virtue of the smile being activated by the face or smile of the other. If the child is reared with a minimum of social interaction and of smiling, he will ordinarily become a less social animal. In the extreme instance of autistic children, as described by Eisenburg and Kanner,[50] they show neither interest nor joy in the presence of their parents.

Autism apart, many withdrawn individuals have, we think, been produced by equally withdrawn parents who have minimized smiling and other affective displays. Interest and joy in the impersonal world, in artifacts, or nature, in motor activity, and in thinking are all possible foci for capturing the energies and affects under such conditions and promoting a monopolistic investment in a social experience.

On the other hand it is possible by a variety of schedules of socialization to produce so extremely extraverted a human being that all of his affect and energy is invested in enjoying communion, in smiling at others, or in being smiled at by others, or in both.

In addition to making it possible to minimize or

[50] L. Eisenburg and L. Kanner, "Early Infantile Autism," *Am. J. Orthopsychiat.* (July, 1956), pp. 556-557.

The Biopsychosociality of the Family

maximize the importance of social interest in the development of each individual, the nature of the smiling response also frees the appearance and disappearance of social interest from dependence on the rhythmic waxing and waning of the hunger drive or the sex drive. Although the smiling response is capable of intensification through social deprivation and satiation through massed exercise, yet intensification and satiation become dependent upon conditions other than the state of hunger or sex drive.

The smiling response as an independent source of reward frees the individual from the requirement of specific body contact and stimulation as a necessary condition of positive reward. In order to enjoy human interaction he no longer requires the breast in his mouth or the vagina to receive his penis. This is not to say that all positive affects can dispense with body contact. The love which is evoked in the child by cuddling, by hugging and kissing, as well as by feeding is vitally important, especially for the very young infant. We do not wish to minimize the importance of body contact, body stimulation, and the satisfaction of hunger for the very young, nor minimize the importance of sexual intercourse for the adult as a source of both pleasure and the evoking of the affects of excitement and joy or love. We do wish to distinguish, however, the consequences of freeing positive affect from necessary dependence on the contact receptors.

The cat must have his fur rubbed to enjoy his own purring. In the infant monkey it is clear that the positive affect is closely tied to the clinging response and the reassuring contact, but it is also clear that it is developing in the direction of joy in the presence of the mother independent of contact. The biological importance of clinging for an aboreal infant whose mother necessarily has to use her arms to swing and support herself is obvious. In the case of birds, the critical response is following rather than clinging, since here it is also important that the infant not be separated from the mother. But since these birds are reared on the ground and not carried on the body of the mother, the imprinted response of the following of the earliest object seen, which is usually the mother, guarantees both some freedom of movement for the mother on the ground as well as the relative proximity of the infant bird.

In the case of the human infant there is a radical change in the biological requirements of the mother-child relationship. There is no clinging (although right after birth and for a short period thereafter the grasping reflex is powerful enough to sustain the weight of the infant) and there is clearly no possibility of following. This does not rule out the possibility that body contact initiated by the mother might not be of great importance as an activator of the smiling response. The smiling response, like the following response of some birds, is primarily mediated through what the infant sees rather than through what he feels through body contact. Body contact is one of the important ways in which distress is reduced in infancy, and since the sudden reduction of distress can be a stimulus to the smiling response, body contact in this way may become a stimulus to the smiling response. The body of the mother, of course, becomes the focus of a complex affect and drive matrix, since it can activate both excitement and joy and can reduce fear, distress, and shame, as well as satisfy hunger and thirst.

But the restriction of positive or negative affects to body contact would seriously impair the social, intellectual, and motor development of the child. The child must be free to explore the world and yet feel safe in doing so. To the extent to which he must have body contact to feel joy and love, he would not be free to satisfy his curiosity in the world about him. He would also be restricted in the kind of social responsiveness which would be possible for him. Thus to be a few feet away from the mother or any other familiar person, to engage in conversation, or to engage in any of the adult variants of human communion, for example, to lecture, to act, to perform before an audience—all of these would constitute frustration unless the smiling-enjoyment response could be emitted to visual stimuli which were at some distance from the child.

The equation of oral interests with every type of human dependence and interdependence has masked the critical role both of the face and of the distance receptors in human communion. Both the face and the tongue are organs of exquisite subtlety of expressiveness. We do not think it accidental that Freud sat behind the patient so that facial interaction was minimized. He shared the almost universal taboo on intimate facial interaction and overweighted the role of the mouth as an instrument of hunger, in symbolizing all human communion. We are arguing that the smile in response to the human face makes possible all those varieties of human communion which are independent of eating and of touching the other.

The purely social wishes of the human being are diverse. They are derivatives of numerous affects complexly organized to create addictions to particular human beings and particular kinds of human communion. While the smile of joy is perhaps the central affect in such a matrix it is by no means the exclusive base of social responsiveness. Humans

226

Silvan S. Tomkins

characteristically are excited by other human beings as well as made joyous by them. They are, on the negative side, distressed, frightened, ashamed, and angered by the deprivation of human interaction as well as by a variety of inappropriate responses from other human beings. At the moment our focus of interest is in the contribution of the smile of joy to the enjoyment of human communion.

Social enjoyments are and can be so diverse partly for the same reason that the objects of man's excitement can be so diverse. Anything which can capture the interest of a human being can also produce the smile of joy. Among this larger set of interests is a very large sub-set of social interests and enjoyments. Every time and every manner in which one human being has excited another either party independently or both can become candidates for social enjoyment. Add to this all the possible transformations which the imagination of an intelligent animal permits and the outcome is a very broad spectrum of social enjoyments.

Social wishes begin with any post-uterine enjoyment which is experienced following the reduction of any unpleasant stimulation such as hunger, pain, crying, or excessively loud sounds, by competing stimulation which is more pleasant or which is similar to that in the womb. Salk[51] has reported that newly born infants cry less and gain more weight when continually exposed to rhythmic sounds which mimic the heartbeat of the mother as it was experienced in the womb. We do not know whether the infant enjoys the womb, although the affective apparatus for the smile has matured by the twenty-eighth

[51] Lee Salk, "The Effects of normal heartbeat sound on the behavior of the newborn infant: implications for mental health," *World Mental Health*, Vol. 12 (1960), pp. 168-175.

week. We do know that there are a variety of intense stimuli to which the neonate is exposed that he does not like, and to which he responds by crying. Since the sudden reduction of any dense stimulation can activate the smile, the infant could enjoy a return to the conditions of the womb if post-uterine stimulation which is similar to intrauterine stimulation can in fact reduce crying and other unpleasant stimulation. Salk's report appears to confirm such a possibility. The reliance on the gentle motion of the rocking crib as a pacifier of distressed infants would appear to be another instance of stimulation similar to that in the womb comforting the neonate.

I have also accidentally discovered further evidence for such a phenomenon. One day I lifted my infant son, who was crying, out of his crib, and held him in my arms while I sat on a chair near his crib. He continued to cry until I stood up, still holding him. I appeared not to have changed the way in which I held him except that I was standing instead of sitting. I then sat down again and immediately he started again to cry. On standing up again, he stopped crying quite as suddenly. I found that this phenomenon was quite reproducible. It suggests, as does Salk's evidence, that when the stimulation closely resembles intrauterine conditions it is sufficient at the very least to reduce the cry of distress, and as the infant gets older, to evoke the smile of joy. Being held in the arms when I sat down would not resemble the support of the womb and the pull of gravity so much as being held by me while I was standing. The same dynamics presumably account for the efficacy of walking the floor with a sick or distressed child, in soothing and quieting him.

Quite apart from the womb, the child comes to experience joy both from relief from distress and from reduction of excitement in being held and supported by the mother, in being fed by her and having her breast in his mouth, in sucking and biting, in tasting the milk from her breast, in being smiled at by her, having body contact with her, in smelling her, in having his body hugged, rubbed, and stimulated by her, in clinging to her and hugging her, in looking at her face, in being looked at by her, and in mutual staring into each others' eyes, in first hearing her voice, before it is understood as speech, in hearing her sing him to sleep with lullabies, and then in hearing her talk, in talking to her, and in engaging in mutual conversation.

As he grows older the nature of his social enjoyment changes, and the father, teachers, and other children become additional objects of social stimulation and reward. He begins to enjoy verbal praise and comment for his efforts even to the point of control and dominance by others. He also now enjoys verbally expressing his feelings, positive and negative, to his mother and others, as well as to be the recipient of such communications. He begins now to enjoy hearing of the experiences of others, their opinions, ideas, values, and aspirations, and to share and compare his experience. He comes to enjoy reminiscing about the past and speculating about the future. He learns to enjoy doing things together, eating together, working together, listening to music together, playing together, cooperatively or otherwise. He comes to enjoy having sexual experience, talking about it and sharing his experiences about it, and daydreaming about it. But above all, throughout his development he enjoys identifying himself first with his mother and father and then with his peers. There are few competitors in the life of the young child to the delight of thinking, acting, speaking, and feeling like his mother and father.

Finally we would distinguish the "attraction" between mother and child based upon the shared smile from the mutual binding tie which develops only gradually and which we have called psychological addiction. Such addiction is as powerful as "biological" addiction. It differs from the latter in being based on negative affect as a deprivation symptom, rather than on pain due to alterations in the composition of the blood stream following abstinence.

Joy is one of the complex of affects organized in particular ways which promotes the formation of psychological addiction. By an addiction, we mean a class of complex affect organizations in which a particular psychological object or set of objects activates intense positive affect in the presence of the object, as well as in the absence of the object so long as the future presence of the object or past commerce with the object is entertained in awareness; and in which the awareness of the absence of the object or any awareness of such a possibility in the future, or circumstance having occurred in the past, activates intense negative affect. Further, the absence of the object becomes the occasion for awareness of the object.

Consider as an example the addiction to the smoking of cigarettes. Such an organization of affect around the activity of smoking meets our criterion of addiction inasmuch as the activity activates interest and/or enjoyment, and the prospect of the activity when one is not smoking also activates interest or enjoyment. The awareness of the absence of smoking or any awareness of the possibility in the future or occurrence in the past activates intense negative affect. Further, these criteria are necessary but not sufficient, since the critical further requirement for addiction is that the absence of the object necessarily reaches awareness. Once having reached awareness, our prior criteria guarantee a combination of suffering and longing until one is again in the presence of the object. There are many interests powered by complex affect organizations which fall short of what we are calling addiction. Thus an individual who would be unhappy about not smoking if it were called to his attention is not addicted by this definition. An individual who is not aware, when he sees his friend light up, that his friend is smoking and that he himself is not smoking is not addicted by our definition. Breaking an addiction is difficult among other reasons because it must become possible to be exposed to the presence or absence of the object of addiction without awareness as an inevitable consequence.

By object, or sets of objects, we refer to any psychological entity—be it person, ideology, activity, or geographical location.

Such an affect organization may be produced in a variety of ways. Our interest at this point is not in an exploration in depth of the nature of addiction, but rather in an examination of the critical role which the affect of enjoyment may play in the formation of addictions.

Simplifying our criterion somewhat, for the sake of ease and clarity of understanding of how addictions may be created, let us assume that the essential feature to be explained is that the presence of the addicted object is intensely rewarding and its absence equally punishing. This is, of course, ordinarily the end point of a series of transformations. No object is inherently evocative of positive affect without limit of time nor is its absence necessarily inherently evocative of intense negative affect indefinitely.

Let us consider one way in which a tight, reciprocal, and enduring two-way interaction can be established between the presence and absence of the object of addiction and intense positive and negative affect. If the absence of the object of addiction is first accompanied by an independent activator of a negative affect such as fear, and this negative affect then is later reduced by the presence of the object of addiction, then the absence of the object of addiction may begin to be experienced as the absence of a reducer of or protector against negative affect, in addition to the object's original positive rewarding characteristics.

An example of such a sequence is Harlow's infant monkeys who run to the surrogate mother for relief from fear activated by a terrifying object. As experience with the mother as a fear reducer continues, her absence can become the occasion, increasingly, of fearful anticipation of the dread events for which her presence has become a specific antidote. The presence of the mother is now a unique reducer of negative affect. The presence of the mother by virtue of her unique ability to reduce fear is now capable of evoking an increment of joy over and above her prior attractiveness. She is now an object of greater joy than before. If now she is removed for a period of time this deprivation can result in an increment of distress since the presence of the mother has assumed added positive significance. Reunion with the mother should now heighten the positive affect since her presence reduces a negative affect of greater intensity and duration than heretofore experienced. We have exaggerated and telescoped a spiral interaction process for ease of understanding. The actual

232

Silvan S. Tomkins

formation of addictions is a more irregular process, with waxing and waning of intensity of positive and negative affect.

However, the central feature of the process is as we have described it. The absence of the object evokes strong negative affect which grows stronger as the object which is missed grows more and more positive, and the presence of the object evokes stronger and stronger positive affect as it reduces more and more intense negative affect which was evoked by absence of the object. The essential conditions are first, that the presence of the object is the unique activator of positive affect as well as the unique remedy for the absence of the object; second, that the absence of the object is the unique activator of negative affect; third, that each activation of positive and negative affect produces an increment in intensity or duration of its inverse which in turn produces a further increment. Thus a mother becomes more and more enjoyable and her absence more and more distressing in turn.

Further, in addiction there are multiple positive and negative affects. The absence of the object of addiction is capable of activating fear, distress, or shame. The presence of the object of addiction evokes excitement as well as joy.

Excitement which leads to joy will not only increase the general tie to the familiar but will heighten interest and curiosity. Butler[52] found that a monkey enclosed in a dimly lit box would press a lever to open and reopen a window for many hours for the chance to look through it. The rate of lever pressing

[52] R. A. Butler, "The effect of deprivation of visual incentives on visual exploration motivation," *J. Comp. Physiol. Psychol.*, Vol. 50 (1957), pp. 172-179.

The Biopsychosociality of the Family

depended upon what there was to see. Much more lever pressing was produced if there was another monkey to see than if there was a bowl of fruit or an empty room. This response appears in monkeys three days old, who are barely able to walk. Some infants will crawl across the floor to press a lever hundreds of times within a few hours.

When Harlow tested his surrogate-mother-reared monkeys under these conditions, they were as interested in the cloth-mother as in another monkey but displayed no more interest in the wire mother than in an empty room. A control group raised with no mothers found the cloth-mother no more interesting than the wire mother and neither as interesting as another monkey.

Thus despite the daily satisfaction of being fed by the wire mother and whatever joy is activated by this experience, yet as judged by the work the infant will do to be able to "look," which is based on the strength of the positive affect of interest, the cloth mother is much more "exciting" than the feeding mother. Repeated activation of joy with the same object has, we think, strengthened the affect of interest with respect to the same object.

We have noted before the way in which the tie to the mother is increased by running to her for help against terrifying objects. Harlow has also shown that separation from the mother also strengthens the positive feelings of the monkey toward its surrogate mother.

That a deepening of addiction can be created by deprivation is shown in Harlow's evidence that infant monkeys raised with a single nonlactating cloth-mother showed a consistent and significant increase in time spent with the surrogate cloth-mother during the first ninety days after having been separated

Silvan S. Tomkins

from their mothers for 9, 30, 60, and 90 days when they were 165-170 days of age.

But if fear and deprivation can strengthen the addiction to the mother, they can also weaken it. Thus if the tie to the mother has not reached a critical positive strength, putting it under stress does not create an addiction but rather it undermines whatever attachment has been achieved. Harlow's evidence with monkeys reared in isolation shows clearly both the importance of primacy and early experience with the mother, and the delicate interplay between positive and negative affect which may swing either in the direction of producing a strong addiction or destroying the existing relationship.

A group of four infant monkeys were raised without physical contact, either with a mother surrogate or with other monkeys. After eight months they were given access to surrogate mothers, either of the cloth variety or of the wire non-pneumatic mothers. Their initial response was fear. In a few days they began to respond like infant monkeys raised on both mothers from birth. They spent about an hour a day with the wire mother and eight to ten hours with the cloth-mother. Normal monkeys raised from birth on the cloth mother, however, spent almost twice as much time with the cloth mother. Another indication of the weaker tie produced by restriction of early enjoyment of the mother was the fact that these "orphan" monkeys were less reassured by the cloth-mother when exposed to a new environment. Finally, in comparison with monkeys reared on the cloth-mother from the start, the early isolated group rapidly lost whatever responsiveness they had acquired once they were separated from the mother. In contrast, monkeys who had been raised on the cloth-mother, retained their attachments and responsive-

The Biopsychosociality of the Family

ness even after eighteen months of separation.

This is in marked contrast to the infant monkeys who had been raised with only a wire-mother. Responsiveness to her disappeared in the first few days after the mother was withdrawn from the living cage. Here again we see that if the tie is weak, frustration will further weaken it rather than strengthen it. In the human mother-infant relationship the dynamics of addiction formation is similar. Each learns to enjoy and "miss" the other, thus creating the tie that binds.

What shall we conclude now about Levy's argument that "for physiological reasons biological mothers will if given the opportunity initiate interaction with their biological offspring with very high probability and the biological offspring if given the opportunity will respond with a very high probability"?

First, it is clear that these two arguments are not equally compelling. The attraction of the mother to her infant is very different from the attraction of the infant to her. One enters the relationship with "biological" mechanisms heavily overlaid with past experience whereas the infant much more closely approximates a pure biological preparation. Both share the same biological mechanisms, but one has in addition used these mechanisms over and over again so that they have been modified by past experience and by social forces. If this learning has made her into an unsympathetic human being she will *not* respond to her infant with love and sympathy with a "very high probability," and consequently her child will eventually respond in kind and not with love. Thus Ainsworth,[53] among many others, has reported that

[53] M. Ainsworth, "The Development of infant-mother interaction among the Ganda," in B. M. Foss, (ed.), *Determinants of Infant Behavior* (London: Methuen, 1961), II.

Silvan S. Tomkins

the only children who fail to develop attachment to a mother are those who have essentially never experienced sufficient attention from their mothers to respond in kind. Harlow has shown that monkeys raised without mothers and without peer experience never learn either to have intercourse or to "mother" children.

Despite this it remains nonetheless true that there is a firm biological base for maternal attraction to the infant, and for social responsiveness in general. But it must not be forgotten that there are equally powerful biological bases for competitors to maternal interests—the lure of excitement about a hundred other possibilities—a career, sexuality, and so on, as well as distress and anger at the enforced responsibility of having to care for the infant.

For the infant the situation is quite different. He too is capable of many affective responses to his new environment. He can be quite excited by *any* stimulus which suddenly bombards him, can smile at *any* familiar stimulus, or at the sudden reduction of any stimulation positive or negative, can cry at any nonoptimal stimulation. It is some time before he can differentiate his mother sufficiently to smile at her and *not* at someone else.

H. R. Schaffer and Peggy E. Emerson[54] reported a longitudinal study on the social behavior of a group of 60 infants during the first 12 months of life. He reported that there is relatively little difficulty in the early months in exchanging the mother for an unfamiliar caretaker:

"As his criterion for the beginnings of object con-

[54] H. R. Schaffer and Peggy E. Emerson, "The Development of Social Attachments in Infancy," Monographs of the Society for Research in Child Development, Serial No. 94 (1964), Vol. 29, No. 3, pp. 3-77.

The Biopsychosociality of the Family

servation Piaget used the infant's orientation towards a missing object, and the parallel development of social and non-social objects is strikingly illustrated by the fact that we found upset on separation from the mother to begin just at the same age that Piaget's infants began searching for objects that had been removed from the perceptual field. Both instances may be said to provide evidence that a permanent object with an independent existence external to the subject had been constructed. The infant after this point is no longer willing to accept *any* environmental attribute that will satisfy his needs but will search until he has found the particular toy or person that now forms the *specific* object of his need."

Schaffer observed children in seven frequently occuring situations: when an infant is left alone in a room, when he is left with other people, when the adult passes by his cot or chair without picking him up, when he is put down after a period on the adult's knee, when he is put outside the house in his pram, when he is left outside shops, and when he is left in his cot at night. By rating the intensity of a child's protests on a four point scale for each of these situations and then combining the scores, he gained an index of the total intensity of attachment.

He found using this index that the seventh month was critical for the emergence of strong attachment, and that the third quarter of the first year was the critical age range. These results confirmed his earlier hospitalization study, since there too separation upset started at the seventh month.

This fits, Schaffer argues, with the fact that Piaget's sensori-motor stage IV, which marks the beginnings of object conservation, first manifests itself at this time. It also fits, Schaffer suggests, with Spitz's

238

Silvan S. Tomkins

findings that in the first six months the smile is re-leased indiscriminately to almost any face-like moving stimulus. Only after six months will the child respond only to familiar faces and not to unfamiliar ones.

The mode of the distribution of fear of strangers occurs about a month after that of the attachment distribution. He presents the following table showing the relationship between attachment to the mother and fear of strangers.

Age at formation of first specific attachment and at emergence of fear of strangers.

Human Month	Attachment N	Fear of Strangers
6	1	0
7	9	2
8	5	8
9	4	8
10	2	4
11	1	0
12	1	0
13 plus	0	1

He suggests that the tendency to seek the company of familiar individuals and the tendency to avoid the company of strangers cannot be regarded as merely the opposite sides of the same coin. An infant may show a high degree of attachment to certain specific individuals and yet very little fear of strangers, or he may have considerable fear of strangers but show only minimal signs of attachment.

Schaffer and Emerson reported that several of their infants invariably cried after father when he passed by yet never after mother, for, he thought, they had presumably learned that the father tended to give way to their demands for attention quite readily whereas mother had consistently refused to do so for fear of "spoiling." He suggests that the eventual intensity of the attachment depends therefore both on the strength of that particular child's need and the extent to which the people around him are prepared to satisfy it.

Schaffer also reports that the mother is by no means the *only* person to whom the infant shows attachment behavior. He found that it is the rule rather than the exception that several individuals are selected as the objects of the infant's attachment responses, that protest at being left in one or another of the seven situations he investigated, was evoked by a number of persons and not just by one. Further, he found that the mother was not always the person to whom attachment behavior was shown most frequently and intensely. She is often the object of most frequent and intense attachment, but there are cases where other people are missed more frequently and more intensely even though the total amount of time that they spend with the child each day may be very much less.

One of his most striking of such examples was an infant who showed far more intense attachment behavior towards the ten-year-old girl living next door than towards the members of his own family—despite the much greater availability of his parents, and despite the fact that the neighbor's daughter never fed him and rarely cuddled him, though Schaffer admits she did carry him around a great deal.

Yet this attachment behavior which occurs in the third quarter of the first year is not entirely new according to Schaffer. In the first six months the infant is reluctant to be left alone by other people. But whereas after seven months the child's crying is set off by the departure of only certain specific individuals, before that time it appears that the company of *anybody,* familiar or stranger, will satisfy the child. Thus a ten month old infant will cry when his mother leaves him in his pram outside the house and will not stop when a stranger tries to comfort him, but will stop only when the mother (or some other specific familiar individual) reappears. In contrast, the five-month-old infant in the same situation will quiet as soon as any passer-by approaches and interacts with him, and will cry again if the stranger leaves. Schaffer reports that all the infants in his longitudinal study showed such indiscriminate attachment before they formed a specific attachment.

Schaffer has also shown that "a prolonged acquaintance with the individual with whom a specific attachment is eventually formed is less essential than the total amount of prior social stimulation received by the infant, irrespective of the source." This is based upon a study of two groups of infants. One of these (which he refers to as the "Hospital group") was obtained from a children's hospital, where the total amount of stimulation, both social and otherwise, received by these infants was limited, and resulted in what Schaffer called "perceptual monotony." "When social interaction did take place it might be with any one of a number of nurses, few of whom stayed for long periods in a particular ward. The 11 infants of this group were, however, visited by their mothers, this being once a week for the majority but several times a week in three of the cases."

"The other group (the 'Baby Home group') had been admitted to an institution because of contact with tuberculosis, necessitating B.C.G. vaccination. There were nine infants in this group, and their mean length of separation did not differ significantly

The Biopsychosociality of the Family

from that of the Hospital group. The age range at time of discharge is also comparable. The nature of their separation experience, on the other hand, differed in two important respects: in the first place no visiting was allowed in the Baby Home and no contact whatever occurred therefore with the mother throughout the course of these infants' stay, and in the second place the amount of stimulation that the Baby Home group received during the separation was far greater than that received by the Hospital group. This was mainly because the ratio of staff to children was very much higher in the Baby Home, with the result that quite a considerable amount of social interaction was experienced by these infants. In the Baby Home, too, however, no infant was looked after by any one particular nurse acting as mother-substitute, care being provided indiscriminately by a large number of nurses."

"After each infant's return home the course of his attachment behavior was plotted." The Baby Home group established a specific attachment to the mother far more quickly than the Hospital group—despite the fact that none of the former infants had had any contact whatever with the mother, whereas all the hospitalized infants saw their mothers at least once a week throughout their stay. The difference between the two groups in this respect reaches a statistical significance level of .02 (Mann-Whitney test), the means of the distributions being 55.0 and 19.7 days respectively."

"In the Hospital group all but one infant took at least four weeks to establish a specific attachment, two took approximately three months to do so, and one infant had still not shown any specific attachment behavior by the time he reached the end of the first year. In the Baby Home group, on the other

242

Silvan S. Tomkins

hand, five of the nine infants developed a specific attachment within five days of returning home and two others did so within the second week."

Schaffer interprets these results as follows: "In the Baby Home a great deal of interaction took place between the infant and his caretakers, and while conditions did not lend themselves to the formation of a specific attachment, a generalized need for social stimulation was fostered. It was this, we must assume, which enabled the infants to establish a specific bond fairly speedily once the environment did supply a constant mother-figure. The Hospital infants, however, had not experienced anything but a minimum of social stimulation, and before being able to form any specific attachments these infants had first to go through a phase of indiscriminate attachment behavior. This took place in all 11 members of this group after their return home, occurring generally within a fairly brief period of this event."

The importance of abundant stimulation from the mother or mother surrogate is highlighted by one of the cases in the Baby Home group which took an exceptionally long time to form a specific attachment. "On his return home this child was looked after by his invalid father, who had to stay at home while the mother went out to work. Both parents were fond of the child, but because of his condition the father was unable to give the child anything but the minimum of care and stimulation, while the mother saw the child for only brief periods each day. Two and a half months after the infant's return home, however, the mother gave up work and devoted all her time to her family, and within a few days the child had developed a strong specific attachment centered exclusively on the mother."

Schaffer argues for a three-stage development of

specific attachment. The first stage is a need for stimulation. The second stage is a need for general social stimulation and the third stage is a need for specific social stimulation: "The infant who at ten months cries for his mother and who at five months cried for the attention of any person, will have cried at three months for almost any form of environmental change."

Harriet Rheingold [55] has also argued that the young infant characteristically searches the environment for stimulation. She has pointed out that for some time the infant is dependent on the parent not only for social stimulation but also for the changing of visual perspective to relieve monotony. So when the adult leaves the child the infant will not be able to vary his own experience sufficiently and will therefore cry.

The paradox of the socialization of the human infant is that he must be cared for by another human being who has *learned* to care more about human beings than about all the possible competitors for human attention. Every human being is innately capable of becoming a psychological "mother," but in order for this to have happened she must herself have been mothered. *If* she has become addicted to human beings in general, it is *then* true, as Levy argues, "for physiological reasons biological mothers will if given the opportunity initiate interaction with their biological offspring with very high probability" and *if* the infant is mothered adequately and for long enough a period of time it is true, as Levy argues, that "the biological offspring if given the op-

[55] Harriet Rheingold, "The effect of environmental stimulation upon social and exploratory behavior in the human infant," in B. M. Foss (ed.), *Determinants of Infant Behaviour* (London: Methuen, 1961), p. 117.

portunity will respond with a very high probability." But the infant will respond at first to *any* stimulation, as well as to *any* mother. Only if the same mother continues to mother him will he become attached and addicted to her, and only if that same mother is the biological mother can it be said he will respond to the biological mother "with a very high probability."

What of Levy's second and third arguments: "without close cognitive and affective interaction (as well as provision of food, shelter, clothing, etc.) with adult members of the species, human infants cannot develop into stable adults and without a reliable production of stable adults a society cannot persist. Such interaction with infants cannot systematically be induced except in biological mothers on a sufficient scale to produce enough stable adults and keep a society in operation."

Levy's contention is somewhat ambiguous since one cannot tell exactly how "stable" adults must be in Levy's opinion for society to persist. Nonetheless the argument is not without force. A great deal of clinical evidence would appear to support Levy's argument. This evidence, while presumptive, is not crucial because of the uncertainty of interpretation of a matrix as complex as is involved in the development of human beings. In the absence of experimental controls one cannot be certain of identifying precisely which one of a hundred factors exerted how much influence in the development of any particular human being. It is for this reason that many of the theoretical questions in this domain have been studied by using animals other than man. While this has permitted experimental control which could not be used in the study of human development, it nevertheless fails to give entirely satisfactory answers to the basic questions about the nature of

The Biopsychosociality of the Family

human development. This is because of the considerable discontinuities between man and his closest ancestors. For what it is worth let us examine the most relevant evidence from the experimental literature on an animal not entirely unlike man.

Harlow's[56] earlier studies of deprived monkeys indicated that the absence of mothering resulted in both male and female monkeys who were incapable of sexual behavior and therefore incapable of reproducing themselves. Such data if applicable to the human species would provide powerful support to Levy's arguments. Subsequent experiments however have revealed that "monkeys deprived of real mothers nevertheless develop normal personalities if they are provided with peers for regular interaction. This occurs whether they have surrogate mothers or not. The infants without mothers begin to play with each other a little later and the maturity of their play is considerably less during the first six months but only slightly less during the next six months than that of mothered infants. In the second year the groups are indistinguishable on the basis of behavior. For monkeys, at least, strong peer relationships can eventually compensate for absence of mother ties." These monkeys did reproduce themselves. Although the combination of mother and peers is required for the optimal development of the monkey according to Harlow's recent results, yet significant compensation is possible through peer interaction.

The relevance of these studies for human development is not clear or certain. Certainly the critical role of language in human development would ar-

[56] Harry F. Harlow, "The nature of love," *Am. Psychologist,* Vol. 13 (1958), pp. 673-685.

gue against the possibility of completely substituting peers for adults as human socializers. Further, the human infant is helpless much longer than the monkey and the possibility of the helpless adequately socializing the other helpless is not reassuring.

There is a wealth of other evidence from experiments with rats, dogs, and many other animals— all of which supports the assumption that the early experience of the young animal may have profound and often irreversible impact on the later development of the animal (though there is also some evidence against such an assumption). Despite such evidence, and its plausibility, it does not seem likely that Levy's assumption about human development will be capable of being answered with great confidence in the near future, either from this evidence or from studies of human infants.

His further proposition that "such interaction with infants cannot systematically be induced except in biological mothers on a sufficient scale to produce enough stable adults and keep a society in operation" seems to me his most powerful single argument. Theoretically this argument cannot be defended— because alternatives presumably are always capable of being invented given an endless development of social science. At the present time, however, and for the forseeable future, the possessiveness of mothers and fathers towards their biological offspring, combined with the widespread belief in the importance of mothering, combined with the improbability of swapping offspring systematically, all tend powerfully to reinforce the biological mother in her role as psychosocial mother. Theoretical alternatives are possible but would seem highly improbable given the convergence of the biopsychosocial forces involved.

The Biopsychosociality of the Family

In this argument Levy seems to me to have discovered a profound generalization, despite the fact that it is argued on grounds which are partly false, and proceeds to conclusions which do not follow with as strict a necessity as he urges.

[24] B. Hokfelt, "Noradrenaline and adrenaline in mammalian tissues. Distributions under normal and pathological conditions with special reference to the endocrine systems." *Acta Physiol. Scand.*, Vol. 25 (1951), pp. 1-134.

G. B. West, D. M. Shepherd, and R. B. Hunter, "Adrenaline and noradrenaline concentrations in adrenal glands at different ages and in some diseases." *Lancet*, 2: (1951), pp. 966-969. See page 156.